Early Day Oil Tales

of

Mexico

Illustrated by Bob Schoenke

🦅 EARLY DAY

OIL TALES OF

MEXICO

BY CHARLES W. HAMILTON

 GULF PUBLISHING COMPANY   HOUSTON

Preface

Prior to my retirement in 1957 I was active in the oil business for over 45 years—first as a geologist and later as an executive—always working in foreign countries or directing foreign exploration and development from this country. In the course of my career I met many different peoples of all classes, races, colors and creeds. A few were saints, many were sinners. Some were teachers, technicians, professionals, merchants, but more were just poor peasants. Many were hard workers in the camp, on the farm, in the shop or in the office. Still others were bandits or guerrilla fighters—all kinds of people motivated by many different impulses—although all had the same common love of living and of family.

Of all my experiences overseas, it now seems that my years in Mexico (1912-1922) were the most intriguing. Those were the days of the great oil boom south of the Rio Grande and, coincidently, a period of almost constant revolution and counterrevolution. The frequent wild wells and burning oil tanks, interspersed with alarms of attacks by insurgents or bandits, payroll ambuscades, and hurricanes, made living in the oil camps and terminals anything but monotonous. All along the Mexican coastal plains for the most part, the weather was hot and sticky and everywhere the fields and woods swarmed with flies, mosquitoes and ticks. Life in Mexico in those days was exciting, adventurous and rewarding.

As a consequence, out of this period of social unrest and oil boom in Mexico have come many unusual tales running the gamut of human emotions. Some of these tales I have recounted over the intervening years to my friends and associates. Most of my listeners appeared entertained though incredulous. In recent years quite a few of my acquaintances have urged me to put my stories in print.

At long last I have accepted the challenge, at least to the point of putting the more colorful stories down on paper. Here then, are my, "Tales of Mexico." For the most part they are personal experiences, or are incidents and episodes that occurred while I was in Mexico and which I believe to be true.

In order to give readers the proper background I shall start off by relating, "How I Got into the Oil Business." Thereafter, the tales about Mexico follow in a more or less orderly sequence as to time and place.

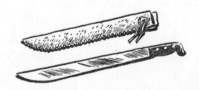

Contents

Early Day Oil Tales

of

Mexico

I

How I Got into the Oil Business

Several years ago I attended the First Ordinary Meeting of the Persian Gulf Branch of the (British) Petroleum Institute. This meeting was held in Kuwait, Arabia. As guest of the Institute's President, Sir Philip Southwell, I sat up front and, in due course, was called upon to speak to the assembled group of some 150 technicians, scientists and engineers. At that time I was an officer of the Kuwait Oil Co., Ltd., Gulf Oil Corporation and many of Gulf's overseas subsidiaries. Having then been active in the oil industry for some 40 years I was looked upon by the youngsters in the business as "the old man." Thus it was that when Sir Philip approached me before the meeting to talk to the group, I asked the pertinent question of what I should talk about. "Just reminisce," was the reply.

Accordingly, when I got up to speak, I said, "From time to time, young fellows such as the majority of you here assembled have asked me how I happened to get into the oil business. The answer is simple in my case, to wit, I got in the oil business because my mother had rheumatism."

Immediately there was a raising of eyebrows and a general quickening of interest among my listeners. Several spoke up and said, "Tell us about it." So with proper apologies, I launched into the story of the rather involved and somewhat unusual circumstances which led to my becoming an oil man.

I was born in 1890 in the country village of Ithaca, Michigan. My father was a merchant and although our family lived comfortably, we were by no means well-to-do. In those days, and especially in our village, domestic help was usually available only during the winter months when farmers were not busy with their planting or harvesting. Hence, sometimes we had help about the house, but more often, none.

I was in high school when my mother developed a severe attack of rheumatism which so crippled her hands and arms that kitchen duties were painful and difficult. My sister was eight years younger than I—too little to be of real assistance. At the time we could not recruit any girls from the outlying farms to help us, so in desperation, Mom offered to teach me how to cook. I readily accepted for her sake and because I rather liked puttering about the kitchen.

So it was that I put on an apron and was inducted into the art of home cooking under the watchful eye of my mother as she sat in her chair near our wood burning kitchen stove, her hands and arms done up in an afghan. As she rocked she explained, day after day, the basic principles of cooking, baking bread, pies, and cakes, making mincemeat, jams and jellies, canning fruits and vegetables, roasting and frying meats, and all the other odds and ends required of a cook in those days before the advent of electric or gas refrigerators—and before there were any frozen foods on the market.

My mother and sister had many a laugh over my ineptness and the ridiculous situations I got into such as the time I put too much rice in the kettle so that when it expanded I had boiled rice in almost every available container; the times my jelly would not jell, etc. Still, we managed, and I had fun. What is more important, I did learn the rudiments of cooking.

That fall we were able to get a "girl" and, in due course, mother's rheumatics got less troublesome; hence, I was excused from kitchen duty.

I didn't know it then, but later the know-how of cooking would greatly influence my career.

After graduating from high school I enrolled in Alma College (Alma is located seven miles from Ithaca), in a general academic course. At that time I had no preconception of what I wanted to do or where I wanted to go. However, I was sure that I did not want to be a small town merchant like my father or a farmer like most of my forebears. College seemed to offer the possibilities of a new and different life.

During my freshman year, out of the blue so to speak, our Congressman obtained for me an appointment to West Point. Through some mix-up the notice of that appointment was delayed so that I had only 10 days from receipt of notice until the examinations at the Academy. Thus, I had no adequate preparation for the tests. At any rate, I failed to qualify.

This failure left me quite dejected because by then I wanted to be a soldier. West Point seemed to me to be the pinnacle-goal of my life. I was distraught and embarrassed by my failure, and I felt I was a disgrace to my folks and community. However, I pulled myself together and returned to college determined to finish my freshman year if I could. Somehow I made the grade.

That summer I sold *The Favorite Medical Receipt Book and Home Doctor* in the thumb of Michigan to earn money enough to take up my sophomore studies in Alma the coming fall. Meanwhile, our Congressman, without our family's knowledge, was working for another appointment to West Point for me—apparently he felt somewhat to blame for the mix-up in my previous notice and my consequent failure. In August 1909 another appointment came through. The examinations were to be held in Columbus Barracks, Columbus, Ohio, the following January.

Again I was in the clouds for this time I knew I would make the grade or bust. So, instead of returning to Alma, I marshaled my meager financial resources and went East to the National Preparatory Academy in Highland Falls, New York. N.P.A. was run by Lieutenant Charles Braden, an ex-army officer, who specialized in preparing boys for the West Point examinations. A file of former West Point entrance examination questions—covering a period of some 50 years—was N.P.A.'s sole curriculum. When I enrolled I was told by Lt. Braden that anyone who took his special West Point preparatory course could be virtually sure of passing the entrance examinations. Nevertheless, he pointed out that appointees with a military background (such as near kin-folk with an honorable military record) had a better chance of being accepted than those who did not have such military background. I had none.

Thus, in Braden's School I boned and crammed with other boys from early morning until late at night, seven days a week, for three months. Never have I studied so hard or so long, either before or since. Finally, January rolled around and it was time to head for Columbus. This time I felt properly prepared for whatever mental and physical tests.

All through the examinations at Columbus Barracks I felt much more sure of myself than I had in the previous grilling at the Academy. I was confident that I could and would make the grade. Hence, when I had returned home, it was a shock to receive, in due course, a terse letter from the authorities at West Point stating that I had failed to pass my entrance examinations. There was no explanation and no announcement of my test grades. My hurt over failure was somewhat alleviated by a telegram from Lieutenant Braden, which said in effect:

"Sorry to learn you have not been accepted for West Point, however, you should know that your grades were higher than some of those accepted."

I knew what Lieutenant Braden meant—namely, that when the chips are down, the candidate with a military background has an edge on the fellow with no such background, whenever their test scores are approximately the same.

Notwithstanding the solace from Lieutenant Braden, I was bitterly disappointed. I felt I was a failure and certainly a disgrace to my parents and community. Although I still wanted to go on to college, I could not bring myself to face my classmates in Alma. Instead, I was determined to seek new collegiate pastures as far away from home as possible. That is what prompted me to enroll in the University of Oklahoma in February, 1910.

Now, you may ask, "Why Oklahoma?" Again, my answer must be involved. First of all, my sixth grade teacher Ivis Parker, had married a University of Oklahoma professor, James Sturgis, and had gone to Norman, Oklahoma to live. As a result, her brother, "Deac" Parker (later, George Parker became editor-in-chief of the Scripps Howard newspaper chain), also went to Oklahoma and enrolled in the University. Because "Deac" Parker went to Norman, "Fat" (Gaylord Nelson), my cousin, also enrolled there. Both "Deac" and "Fat" were a few years older than I, and I idolized them. Both had largely worked their way through college, so it was only natural for me to feel that if they could do it, I could, too.

After defraying the expense of my Highland Falls prep schooling, and transportation to and from, I was financially busted. However, father came to my rescue when I announced my intention of going to Oklahoma, by advancing me $100.

On reaching Norman, I matriculated at the University as a sophomore and declared my major as chemistry (Why? because my cousin had majored in chemistry). That semester I did chambermaid work in the Sturgis home for my room and paid $3.00 a week for board at a nearby boarding house.

However, in spite of my meager expenditures, the nest egg loaned me by my father was completely gone by June, so I could not go home for the summer holidays. In order to eat, I got a job in Norman on a construction gang laying city pavements. My particular job of tending the concrete mixer was hot work but the pay was good.

That summer I heard a rumor that the Oklahoma Geological Survey in conjunction with the U.S. Geological Survey was going to put a field party into the northeastern part of the state to map surface formations along the edge of the oil fields. What really intrigued me though was that the O.U. students recruited for this joint party would be paid $50 a month while in the field and would be given four hours of school credit for the summer's work. After a skimpy first year in Alma and the loss of six months academic work while getting ready for West Point, I needed school credits—all I could get. I felt I had to somehow join that joint geological survey party.

When I applied to Dr. C. N. Gould (Director of the Oklahoma Geological Survey) and to Dr. D. W. Ohern (head of the School of Geology) for a job on the joint survey, they both discouraged me. They said I did not have enough geology and, furthermore, they had many student applicants who were better qualified than I. In fact, they told me in my first interview that all field positions were filled. Nevertheless, I persisted, and at long last, one evening some 10 days later Dr. Gould (I think it was he) said, "Hamilton, you are a persistent lad. We've told you time and again that all regular field jobs are filled—however, one opening in the party still remains open—can you cook?"

"Yes," I replied. "I can cook, in fact I am a good cook—I was taught by my mother and can do, with some practice, all sorts of plain cooking, including bread, pies and cakes."

Then and there I was hired.

That summer I cooked for about two months and then

graduated to field work as a rodman. I found I liked geology and determined to make it my vocation. Before the season ended Dr. Gould offered me a job as janitor in the Oklahoma Geological Survey office (location in Norman on the University grounds), explaining that I could do my chores out of class hours. In order to cinch this position, I informed Dr. Ohern that I intended to change my major from chemistry to geology.

In the course of the next school year I was advanced in the O.G.S. from janitor to rewriting and editing. The next summer (1911) I again hired out as cook for a field party— this time for the U.S.G.S. party mapping the brown coal (lignite) outcrops in North Dakota and Montana. And again I was promoted to rodman after a few weeks over the stove.

I continued to work for the O.G.S. during my senior year at the University. In the spring of 1911, E. L. DeGolyer had come back to Norman from Mexico to complete his thesis for his degree. In Mexico he was Chief Geologist and head of the Land Department for the Mexican Eagle Oil Co. I met Mr. DeGolyer while he was in Norman, and, in fact, we became good friends. I told him that I thought it would be interesting to do geological work in Mexico when I graduated. He replied, "Write me all about yourself next spring." Accordingly, in the late spring of 1912 I made formal application to DeGolyer for a job as field geologist with his oil company in Mexico. My application was accepted, and the day after getting my sheepskin, I climbed aboard the train at Norman and headed for Tampico. Thus, in June, 1912, I began a career in the foreign oil business—all because my mother had rheumatism and taught me how to cook.

My small audience of Petroleum Institute members in Kuwait—mostly British—listened attentively, although I sensed a feeling of incredulity over the maze of circumstances which had shaped one American's destiny.

2

Indians of Mexico

After arriving in Mexico in June, 1912, my first several years of field work brought me into close contact with the Indians of the Huasteca and the Isthmu de Tehuantepec. I lived with them in their pueblos and campos. We ate the same food, slept in similar cots under the same thatch and enjoyed common chit-chat. I learned the hard way that the male Indian is unpredictable and vicious when drunk, but when sober a hard working, simple, honest fellow, good to his family and to his fellowmen. (The lazy louts tourists sometime see along the streets and highways of Mexico are more often than not Mestizos.) Under normal circumstances the Mexican Indian in the country will share his food and lodging with a stranger. Many times my Indian friends have refused to accept payment of any kind for their unstinted hospitality.

The great Indian dynasties which predated the invasion of the Conquistadores (1517-1521) developed a civilization and culture in Mexico far superior to that of the Indians in the United States and Canada. The ruins of these Mexican temples and gods are found in many places on the plateau and coastal plains of Mexico and Central America. Their customs and culture persist to this day.

Unlike the Indians north of the Rio Grande, the Indians of Mexico were never absorbed by European stock. Although they were conquered and dominated by the Spaniards, and subsequently felt the imprint of the French, German, American and English settlers and adventurers, the Mexican Indian has emerged as a positive ethnic group and still remains the backbone of Mexican political, economic, social and cultural life. Almost without exception, the great leaders of Mexico over the past 150 years have been either full-blooded Indian or Mestizos.

The dress, customs and food of the Mexican Indian and the borderline natives of Guatemala are distinctive—in many ways, quite different from that of other Indians now living elsewhere in North and South America.

Huasteca

All the oil fields of Mexico have been found in Indian country, with many of the largest oil wells on lands still owned by descendants of the Aztecs. The country around Tampico, Panuco, and Tuxpam is referred to as the Huasteca (Huaxtica), the name given to the Indians of the vast region of the Oriental of Mexico lying between the Gulf of Mexico and the Sierra Madre mountains. Panuco is so-called from the name of an Indian chief of the time that river was discovered by Hernandez de Cordoba in 1516. Tampico is a Huastecan word meaning "place of the dogs." Tamesi (Tamesin) is the name of a river which empties into the Panuco near Tampico, is another Huastecan word signifying "place of many alligators." Tuxpam (Tuxpan) is Aztec for "where rabbits abound."

Dress

In the hinterland of the Tierra Caliente (hot country) of Mexico life is simple and so is the native dress. The Indian men customarily wear a wide-brimmed conical-peaked straw hat, a white cotton coat-shirt and a pair of white cotton drawer-like pants tied around the ankle to keep out the insects, and sometimes open leather sandals. The dress of the Indian women usually consists of a colored cotton rebosa (a sort of scarf worn either over the head or around the shoulders), a loose sleeveless white cotton blouse tucked into a heavy cotton knee length skirt embroidered in a pattern of varicolored wool yarn, no stockings, no undergarments (except possibly a slip) and no sandals.

For added protection against the cold, or in rainy weather, the adult hot-country Indian wears the brightly colored wool serape. When the serape is used for warmth or for protection from rain, it is worn over the head with the head protruding through a slit in the middle of the serape. This covers the shoulders and upper body to below the waistline. At night it is often used as a blanket although it covers only the head and upper body. In other words, the serape doubles as a coat, a poncho and a blanket, for men and women alike.

Clothes for Mexican Indian children are even simpler. Customarily the boy and girl toddlers wear no clothes at all

until three or four years old. Then, for the next four or five years, the little girls wear a simple cotton slip extending from the shoulders to just above the knees, while the boys wear only a white cotton sleeveless shirt which usually does not extend below the navel. Not until the children approach adolescence are they clothed like their parents.

Notwithstanding the simple dress (or lack of it) of the hinterland Mexican Indians, there is no sense of immodesty or accentuated immorality either at play or work. There is no segregation of sexes among the youngsters. In fact, whole families literally live together from birth until death—often in one common room—sometimes for several generations.

Nursing Babies

The Mexican Indian mother in the hot country frequently nurses her baby until the child is five or six years old. I've been told that the Indian women believe they will not become pregnant so long as their current baby is being suckled. At any rate, it is not unusual to see a mother nursing a toddler standing by her side as she sits on a bench or chair doing her mending or preparing food for the grown-ups.

When an Indian mother is working in the field or walking along the trail between villages, her infant is carried on her back in a sling made from a rebosa. At feeding time, the rebosa is hitched to the side and the baby is nursed at the breast without the mother stopping whatever she may be doing. More than once I have seen a mother not even bother to hitch the rebosa-held baby to her side but, without breaking her stride, simply throw one of her breasts up to her shoulder where the baby could reach the nipple.

Delousing

Among Indians, head lice is so common that there is no shame attached to it. However, periodically an attempt is made to get rid of the pests. Usually that is a family affair as each member lines up one behind the other—the littlest in front, the tallest behind—each intent on delousing the one in front. Such a family effort in front of a native abode in the country is not uncommon on a Sunday or holiday and is usually accompanied by much laughter and song from all members of the party.

Bathing

The hot-country Mexican Indian, away from cities and towns, is inherently clean, and bathes daily if possible. Men and women coming in from the fields will often bathe in a stream or lake before going to their homes. In such case the men and boys bathe in the nude while the women and girls squat and slosh around in their slips. Several times, as I was returning in the late afternoon from doing geological field work, I would take to a stream for a bath in the nude only to be joined in the water by a giggling group of young Indian boys and girls—laughing at me for my sense of modesty.

Corn

The staff of life for all the Indians of Mexico and Central America is maize. All the descendants of the Aztecs and the Mayas are corn eaters. Corn is the basic ingredient of every meal for young and old. In the junglelands it is consumed as *bosoli*, elsewhere the corn is partaken of as a *tortilla* or the *gordito*.

The first stages of preparation for both bosoli and the tortilla are similar. Dry corn is soaked overnight in a strong lye water made from wood ashes. When the outer hull of the corn has been sufficiently softened, the swollen kernels are rinsed in fresh water several times. Then a handful of this wet corn is placed on a stone *metate* (a curved slab of lava rock having short sturdy legs) and ground to a *massa* (dough) with a lava rock rolling pin. This grinding operation may take several hours to prepare enough massa for one day's meals for a single family.

To make bosoli, the raw massa is set aside and allowed to ferment slightly. It is then balled and wrapped in banana leaves and deposited in a cool place until it is needed. The Indian workmen carry these wrapped cannon-balls of bosoli into the jungle and when hungry they break off a piece of the sour tasting massa into a half gourd of water, stir and drink it down. I've known my mozos in the Isthmus de Tehuantepec to maintain their vigor and health for six working days each week on nothing but bosoli for food.

Tortillas are made from the same massa as bosoli, but unfermented. To make the tortillas, Indian women pluck off a piece of fresh massa in their water dampened hands and pat it out flat and round like a small pie crust. When it is almost translucent-thin, it is slapped onto a dry, hot ceramic griddle and allowed to bake on both sides until it curls away from the hot surface. Then the tortilla is done. Generally, it is served without salt or butter, but hot from the fire.

Indians prefer white corn to any other because it makes for white tortillas. They also like fine grained tortillas which are possible only if the massa is repeatedly ground and re-ground. The result is a tortilla as white and as dainty as a napkin.

In the Indian country of Mexico the tortilla is both food and an instrument for conveying food from the plate to the mouth. It is usually torn apart and passed directly into the mouth or can be rolled into a small cone to scoop up eggs, beans, meat or whatever. One can get so dexterous using tortillas that no fork or spoon is necessary to eat a complete dinner from *sopa* to *dulce* without soiling one's hands.

One important characteristic of tortillas is that they are never too old to be edible in some form or other. They can be reheated until scorched, and then they taste like parched sweet corn. They can be dropped in deep fat and salted until they taste like cocktail *fritos*. They can be smothered in hot chile sauce and wrapped around meat or cheese to make delicious *enchillados* or they can be dropped into deep hot fat to make *tacos*. There are almost innumerable ways to make old tortillas into succulent and sustaining dishes. Incidentally, the corn massa is also used to make *tamales, gordo,* and many other tasty items.

From forest and field the hot-country Indians of Mexico and Central America can get or grow everything their bodies need in the way of food and drink. Each family can be self-sufficient in the way of corn, coffee, beans, eggs, meat, fowl, fats, fruit, melons and chile peppers—and what they don't grow they can pluck wild from the forest. No native peoples anywhere have a more varied and better balanced diet than these descendants of the Aztecs and Mayas.

3

Oil Finding in Mexico

Natural asphalt and seepages of heavy black oil were
known to man in Mexico as early as the pre-Cortez
days. The Mayas and Aztecs called it *chapapote*. There is no
certain evidence that the Indians of Central Mexico ever
made use of chapapote in building their temples and pyramids but their cousins in the hot country all along the Gulf
of Mexico caulked their canoes with it.

On March 10, 1826, Capt. G. F. Lyon, R.N.F.R.S., newly
appointed Commissioner for the Real de Monte and Bolaños
Mining Companies enroute to the interior of Mexico, crossed
the bar of the Panuco River on the brig *Perseverance* out of
England. After spending some five weeks in the new town of
Las Tamaulipas, the old town (Pueblo Viejo) and the village
of Tampico, Capt. Lyon proceeded on the examination of the
River Panuco in a large wooden dugout canoe. In his *Journal
of a Residence and Tour in the Republic of Mexico in the
year 1826*, published in 1828, Capt. Lyon says:

Passing for some time the banks of San Pedro, we came to the Estero de Chila, another extensive rancho, the cattle of which were either grazing or lying under the shade of the trees close to the water's edge. On this estate, at about three or four miles from the river, is a large lake, from whence I understand that the petroleum which is brought in great quantities to Tampico is collected. It is here called Chapapote, and is said to bubble from the bottom of the lake, and float in great quantities on the surface. That which I saw at different times was hard and of good appearance and was used as a varnish, or for covering the bottom of canoes; the general price was four reals (half a dollar) for a quintal (100 pounds).

So far as I know Lyon's *Journal* is the first authentic report of the commercial use of seepage oil in Mexico—and that report lay fallow in the world libraries for 75 years before any considerable commercial production of petroleum was obtained in Mexico from drilled wells.

In 1869 a hole 125 feet deep was drilled for oil in what later came to be known as the Furbero field, and a few years later a Mexican company built a small "tea-kettle" refinery at Papantla to treat seepage oil. A Boston concern drilled several shallow holes near Cerro Viejo in the Tuxpam region in 1880-1883 without finding commercial production. Thus it was not until the turn of this century that the commercial oil possibilities of Mexico became apparent. These "discoveries" were the result of drilling wells at or near large seepages of chapapote, which had been observed by Capt. Lyon about 75 years earlier.

British interest found commercial production in the Isthmus de Tehuantepec, where S. Pearson and Sons, Ltd. were building a railroad. Pearson's engineers and construction crews had observed seepages of petroleum and sulphurous water in some of the large salt marshes along the right of way. These were believed to be associated with subsoil salt domes, which had suddenly received much world-wide publicity as a major oil reservoir with the discovery of Spindletop field in Texas. All of the early oil fields in the Isthmus were in fact found on or around the flanks of salt intrusives.

Shortly after the Isthmus discoveries Pearson (who later became Lord Cowdrey) organized the Cia Mexicana de Petroleo El Aguila SA (Mexican Eagle Oil Company) and started drilling around the seepage areas of Tierra Amarilla, Potrero del Llano, Tanhuijo and Tumbadero in northern Veracruz to the west and north of Tuxpam. In 1908 the famous Potrero del Llano No. 4 gusher came in wild—one of the world's largest wells.

Intrigued by the oil seepages along the shore of Lake Tamiahua between Tuxpam and Tampico, the Pennsylvania Oil Co. drilled several wells on the property known as San Diego. One of these wells went wild, burned and cratered in 1904. That was *Dos Bocas* which served to convince the oil fraternity that surface chapapote was a definite clue to subsurface petroleum deposits.

Several California oil men became interested in the oil possibilities of Mexico shortly after commercial production was found in the Los Angeles area (1890). E. L. Doheny and his associates concluded that the chapapote of Mexico was the same stuff as the *la brea* of California. They also noted that *la salina* was the Spanish term for a salt marsh and that *el petroleo* in Mexico meant petroleum. So they combed the maps of Mexico for names of places such as Chapapote, La Salina and El Petroleo and in 1903 sent down their engineers for a first-hand look at these places. It was the many oil seepages around Ebano, Juan Casiano and Cerro Azul that led to the discovery of those great oil fields.

It was not until 1908 that the science of geology was employed in Mexico to find oil and actually it was some years later before the geologist was really accepted there.

All the early commercial discoveries of oil in Mexico resulted from drilling near surface seepages of oil, or around the salt marshes.

4

Vignettes of
Mexican Oil Field Life

Fresh out of college, a tenderfoot geologist, I got my first field assignment in Mexico during the early summer of 1912 in the so-called South Country oil fields of northern Veracruz. My instructions were to proceed from Tampico to Tanhuijo (sometimes spelled Tanguijo) by launch and from there by decauville railway to San Marcos, Alazan and Potrero del Llano, all properties of the British oil company which had employed me.

Tanhuijo was not much of an oil field—just a handful of wells that produced as much salt water as oil. However, it was the training camp for all the company's new cable tool drillers and also was the head of water navigation for the company's material movement from both Tuxpam and Tampico. The material was transported overland via the narrow gauge railways on small 4-wheel platform cars pulled by mules—a distance of some 40 kilometers from Tanhuijo to Potrero. Hence Tanhuijo, in its day, was a very important terminal.

On my arrival I reported to Mr. Dewey, the general superintendent, who assigned me a bed in the guest house and suggested that I remain in camp for a few days to get acquainted and to get outfitted for the field. After depositing my bags I strolled about camp and generally became familiar with the lay of the land. There seemed to be a sort of orderly confusion everywhere. Oil field pipe and equipment and general stores were being unloaded from barges at the river docks, men were shouting, cars were being loaded for the long mule haul over the railway, steam boilers at the drilling rigs were constantly blowing off, and walking beams swayed up and down as the drilling engines chugged and snorted. Every now and then out of the wells would spew a black mess as the tools or bailer were withdrawn. The ground around the wells being worked over was an oily mire and the rig-crews were black from head to foot with oily muck.

I was fascinated by the hurly-burly scene—the smell of mud, sulphur gas and oil and the jungle land which lay all about. I was especially intrigued by the native village which sprawled below the guest house in a depression across the railway tracks. I could look down from the guest house porch and see the narrow muddy streets, lined by flimsy bamboo-palm thatched saloons, honky tonks and restaurants, all thronged by Mexican peons in their colorful dress. As night fell the confusion in the camp lessened, then died, but as the lights were turned on there was a crescendo of voices and music from the village. This was payday. Another Saturday night orgy was in the making.

About ten o'clock I turned in. At that hour no one else was in the guest house, though from the wearing apparel and personal effects scattered around it was obvious that other men lived there. Sleep did not come quickly for although I was dog tired, everything was so strange and confused that I lay awake listening and wondering. However, I must have dozed off, for suddenly I was startled by the sound of rough American voices around my cot. They were voices of angry, drunken men. I kept my eyes closed.

"Who is this kid in my bed?" said one hostile voice. The others protested they didn't know.

"Hey, kid, who are you and what are you doing on my cot?" said the first fellow.

"Get up or we'll throw you out," said another. The others mumbled agreement, cursing me the while.

Fearing to keep my eyes closed any longer, I stood up and in a calm voice which I hoped was quite convincing stated just why I was in that particular cot. I saw by the dim light which shone in the room from the porch that these four fellows were drillers still in their oily clothes from one of the rigs. I topped off my story with an explanation of having been assigned this very bed by the general superintendent himself.

The leader of the four men thought for a moment then said, "Well, kid, we'll forget all about your bedding down in my bunk if you'll come with us to the native village and buy us a round of drinks." I was in no mood to resist so as soon as I pulled on my clothes the five of us wound our way down the hill ond over the tracks to the nearest cantina.

The bar of the cantina opened onto the street and customers stood on duck boards above the mud under the inky black sky and hoisted their drinks. Gasoline lamps hanging from the rafters over the bar reflected their eerie yellow light on the faces of the rough crowd of Mexicans and Americans —some standing with glass in hand, others milling by.

As my new friends and I stood there drinking, I turned and gazed over the moving mass of humanity. Suddenly, I saw a native coming down the street with a long knife in his hand—he was obviously *boracho* and intent on killing someone. As he came closer he glanced at my friends and evidently

recognized the ringleader as his victim. He raised his arm and hurried toward the American driller next to me, fully intent upon stabbing him in the back.

I quickly nudged my newly-found friend, saying, "There's a crazy peon with a knife coming up behind you—move quickly or you'll get it."

Without saying a word or giving any sign that he'd heard me, the big, half-drunk driller turned and swung his huge fist which fortunately made solid contact somewhere on the head of his would-be assassin. The peon fell in the mud like a log, whereupon his intended victim reached over, picked up the knife, heaved it out into the muddy street, and kicked the peon into the same mire. He then turned and went on drinking as though nothing had happened. Soon the assassin picked himself out of the mud and staggered off muttering.

That experience, coupled with the raw whiskey, left me al-most sick with fright.

A few moments later the boss driller finished his drink, then said, "Thanks, buddie. Let's go inside and watch the monte game for a while." (Monte is a Mexican game some-what similar to faro. It is played with Mexican cards which are totally different from the conventional American deck. The players bet on each turn of the dealer's cards. The deal-ers are usually professionals.) So we went inside the building adjoining the bar.

There were billiard and pool tables around the floor, but on one side were several long tables end-to-end. The dealer and his helpers sat behind the tables with their backs to the wall while the players stood in front of the tables with their backs to the door and the onlookers. The room was crowded. My friends elbowed their way across it and up to the monte table—I followed.

I watched the game for maybe a half hour, fascinated by the play and the huge bets of my friends and several well-dressed Mexican players. With the turn of each card the dealer would call out the spot, such as, "El Ray rojo" (the red king), "Hombre a Caballo" (man on a horse), etc. It was terribly exciting. Now and then, the dealer would order drinks on the house for the players. The place was full of noise, confusion and tension. Again I was standing next to the big boss driller, the one who had accused me of occupying his bed. After a while I turned to watch the goings on in the room, for everything was so new and strange. All of a sudden, I saw that crazy peon again, staggering in the doorway with a naked machete in his hand. I said to my friend, "Here he comes again—with a machete this time."

Calmly the big man leaned across the table and plucked a billiard cue from the rack, then turned and in a single swift motion, cracked it over the peon's head. The man went down like a felled ox, head bleeding and machete slithering away over the floor. My friends looked down and, when they saw the peon was badly hurt, decided that we had better get back to camp, lest we all land in the hoosegow.

So ended my first night in an oil camp in Mexico.

My first field assignment in Mexico took me from Tanhuijo to San Marcos to geologize that hacienda. It was a one man job and hence I had to live off the country, which was complicated by the fact that I knew no Spanish. Since the geology of this property had been done by my predecessors, I knew I had to turn in a factual and convincing report. Without an interpreter my getting about would certainly be difficult. But with my handy vest pocket Spanish-English dictionary and the confidence of a young geologist fresh out of college, I was determined to do an expeditious and efficient job.

Each day I rode through the hills and walked the *quebradas* (stream beds—usually dry) looking for outcrops of rocks. When I did find an outcropping, I studied the dip and strike of the bed, and wrote up a description of the exposure in my notebook. Inasmuch as I was working out of one base, my goings and comings were seen by many of the local villagers. After several days I began to notice that a young native girl, maybe fourteen or fifteen years old, would be by the road whenever I passed. Naturally I wanted to be friendly and so called out, "buenos dias, Senorita, como esta?" She would smile rather timidly then scamper toward her house.

After a few days of such greetings, one evening the girl stood her ground and said in Spanish that her mamma wanted to talk to me. She had to illustrate with signs before I understood what she was saying.

At any rate I turned my horse and rode up to her house to talk with mamma. The mother beamed all over and shook my hand when I had dismounted. Then she patted the young girl on the back and launched into a flood of Spanish which at first I didn't understand. However, with the help of my dictionary and signs from mamma and daughter, I made out the story.

First of all mamma wanted to know whether or not I was married and how long I would be working in and around San Marcos. When she learned I was single, working alone and would be on this job for several weeks, she candidly proposed that I buy her comely, virgin daughter for 500 pesos. The girl would do my cooking, laundry, sewing and keep my bed warm for as long as I wanted. I could see the girl was a willing accessory to the plot, and I must admit it was a tempting proposition, especially as I was lonely and needed someone to help teach me conversational Spanish.

Still, the thought of "buying" a girl stuck in my craw; too much like slavery. So I didn't buy, giving as my excuse that I didn't have that kind of money and that my fiancee back home wouldn't understand. Instead, I compromised by giving mamma my laundry to wash and mend for which I paid somewhat more than the current rate. Apparently there were no hard feelings over the "no sale"—daughter continued to smile and call salutations as I rode by and mamma gave me an embrazo whenever I came within arms length.

When I finally finished my project and left San Marcos, mamma and daughter were still my good friends—nothing more.

About a year before World War I, "Lord Bill" arrived in Tampico with letters from the London office of the largest British oil company in Mexico instructing the local management to give this young man every opportunity and facility to learn the oil business from the grass roots up.

Lord Bill's father belonged to the peerage of England, and was presumably a substantial shareholder in one or more of Lord Cowdrey's enterprises—or maybe he had connections with the Ministry of Fuel and Power. At any rate, there was reason to believe that high influence had brought Lord Bill to Mexico.

He arrived with a vast number of trunks and valises containing clothes for every occasion, both day and night, sportswear, riding clothes, saddlery, a small library, guns and fishing tackle, shoes, boots and hats galore. He had everything but work clothes for the oil camps. However, in spite of his letters and his baggage, Lord Bill was well liked by all the English and Americans in both office and field. He was the rugged athletic type—handsome, full of good humor and always with an engaging smile. Lord Bill never pulled either rank or title, while in Mexico, even though there were times when he must have felt miserable from being the butt of the practical jokes and banter of his roughneck associates.

Lord Bill spent a few days in the main office in Tampico before being sent to the oil camps. His initial field assignment was Tanhuijo. There, for the first time, he was exposed to American roughnecks on the derrick floor by day and around the poker table by night. He was anxious to learn the great American game of poker and did so eventually, but only after losing all of his baggage and personal effects. As the result, the American drilling crews in the South Country were decked out in custom-tailored English clothes seldom seen on rawboned Texans—but somehow their cowboy boots looked out of keeping with the rest of the ensemble. As a matter of fact, Lord Bill was so "cleaned" at poker that the boys took pity on him and loaned him their dungarees and shirts until his next remittance arrived.

Tanhuijo was an edge oil field, and thus its wells produced as much water as oil. Drilling was done by cable tools and the holes were difficult to complete. For these reasons the British company used the field as a training ground for newcomers, especially drilling crews. Every new crew, recruited from the States, was required to spend weeks or even months working on the Tanhuijo wells before being assigned elsewhere. Some of the holes had been reworked so many times that the recurring spillage and blowouts had turned the area around these wells into an oily quagmire. At his own request Lord Bill was given a job as rig helper on one of the rework jobs.

He reported to the drillers in charge and was told that first of all he should watch the other crewmen, observe what they did and how they handled the various pieces of drilling equipment and pipe, and then ask questions about operations which he didn't understand.

After wandering about the boilers, the engine and the mud pits, he came up on the derrick floor and became fascinated by the walking beam going up and down and the driller's handling of the temper screw clamped onto the drilling cable and tools. The driller relaxed on the lazy bench, now and then giving the screw a twist to lower the cable and tools down in the hole. When the screw ran out, the tools were pulled out and a bailer was run to clean out the cuttings in the bottom of the hole. With every trip of the bailer, oil and muck spewed over the derrick until the crew resembled slinky black scarecrows dripping with oil from head to foot. But Lord Bill stayed with it, asking all sorts of questions as to why they did this and that.

After bailing, a fresh bit was put on the tools and lowered into the hole. The cable hummed over the crown block. The bull wheel spun so fast the axles got smoking hot. When the driller was satisfied the tools were back on bottom he sat on the top of the lazy bench, with hand on temper screw, and started the walking beam in motion, up and down, up and down. Now and then he'd lower the tools a few inches, in order to keep the bit on bottom.

Lord Bill was curious as to how the driller could tell when the tools were on bottom and when they were off bottom. The driller told him he could "feel" whether or not the tools were on bottom by the vibration in the temper screw. Lord Bill put his hand on the screw but said he couldn't get the feel.

At last the driller said, "Well Lord Bill, the only way for a beginner to learn the feel is to get up on the walking beam."

Lord Bill persisted that he wanted to learn, so the engine was shut off while he crawled up onto the walking beam and out over the end to which the drilling cable is attached. There he sat astride with one hand holding onto the drilling cable. When he was all set the driller slowly started the engine and the walking beam began its up and down movement. With each down stroke the driller asked Lord Bill if he could "feel" the tools hit bottom. Lord Bill was nonplused—sometimes he said he could "feel" and other times not as he bounced up and down on that squared and splintery wood beam. Every now and then the driller would race the engine causing the walking beam to plunge up and down like a bucking bronco, with poor Lord Bill hollering "she's on bottom" as he bounced higher and higher, while he clung onto the wire line with both hands to keep from being pitched onto the derrick floor.

The crew members were in stitches from laughing. To them it was quite a joke, notwithstanding their victim was in real distress from rough splinters and bone-jarring jolts. Lord Bill did not call quits, even though he could see that the boys were pulling his leg. After a cruel few minutes or so, the driller slowed down the engine to its normal speed and lowered the tools so that the jar on bottom was evident to Lord Bill. When he'd got the bottom feel, Lord Bill was allowed to descend to the derrick floor where he was boisterously congratulated by all the crew for learning the know-how the hard way.

From that day forth Lord Bill was no longer plagued by the American drilling crews—he had made good—they were pals.

Lord Bill stayed on in Mexico, moving from camp to camp and from job to job, until there were rumors of war in Europe. When he left the fields he was given a send-off by a host of friends of all nationalities such as few men ever had. However, he went away without any of the elaborate and varied trappings he arrived with. In their place he carried with him a comprehensive knowledge of the oil business in Mexico from the grass roots up and also the best wishes of all his rough oil field associates.

I understand that Lord Bill afterwards held down a responsible post in the Admiralty during World War I.

During the heyday (1912-1922) of the oil boom in Mexico, payday camp life was rough and the oil men likewise. Money came easy and went the same way. There was liquor, gambling and women for anyone who wanted to pay, usually sampled in the order mentioned. All were conveniently available in "shanty towns," outside the main camps. However, the American roughnecks, more often than not, on payday had their own bottles in camp and did some serious gaming in the bunkhouses or club before seeking other diversions.

Dice were thrown on the billiard table—up against the cushion or "no dice." One pay night at Potrero del Llano I saw $10,000 in gold wagered on a single pass of the ivories. Rough men, packing six-guns, stood around the table in a smoke filled room, breathing down one another's necks at each throw of the dice. It was not unusual for a loser to pledge his horse and saddle, even his store clothes, before calling it quits.

Poker was the prime favorite with most drilling crews, geologists and engineers. Commonly these were table-stake games. Six or seven men sat around a blanket-covered board table, each with a six-gun on his hip or laid alongside his chips. No strangers were allowed in these games. Everything was straightforward and aboveboard or else someone got hurt. Any player could declare before the cards were dealt how much he was playing behind his chips and thus could be called for any part of his declared roll as well as the chips in sight.

I remember the poker luck of one young undergraduate geologist who had been temporarily employed during the college summer vacation. His pay was $100 a month, but he liked to gamble and sat in the smaller camp games every Saturday night when he was not in the field. When it was time to go back to school he was flat broke. However, he borrowed a stake for his final poker fling the night before he was to leave. I watched the game. Lady Luck was by his side. When quitting time came he had the cash equivalent of more than six months work after paying all his debts.

Once back in 1913 I got into trouble in a poker game at Los Naranjos for taking exception to some remarks that a tool dresser made about a fellow geologist seated at the table. Heated words followed and both the tool dresser and I laid our six-guns on the table. The situation could have gotten out of hand had it not been for the camp superintendent by the name of Roberts. (The tool dresser worked directly under

Roberts and, although I was a geologist, I was responsible to Roberts while in camp.)

Roberts said, "Boys, put away your guns—we'll have no shooting, but you soreheads can fight it out with fists tomorrow (July 4th) in front of all the men in camp."

Well, with that we cooled off and continued our game. I didn't sleep well that night for the tool dresser chap was rugged and big; however, I had let myself in for something I could see no way out of. The next morning Roberts called me into his office and said that he wanted me to deliver an urgent message to a camp some twenty miles distant explaining that he could not very well ask any of his drilling crews to make the round trip on horseback on a holiday. Since it was raining I could not do any field work anyway, so I might as well spend my time in the saddle as sitting around camp. I told Roberts that I was free to do as he requested, but I couldn't leave camp until after the fight with the tool dresser. He said rather curtly, "I will square your affair with the tool dresser. In this camp you both answer to me—so get going."

I went and didn't return until the next day. When I came across the tool dresser, he was friendly and apparently quite satisfied with the outcome of our affair.

That summer while I was working out of the same oil camp, with another geologist assisting me, our field work was halted by rains. The two of us were seated on a bunkhouse porch overlooking the river, when along came a tool pusher by the name of Tony Williamson. Now Tony was a rough diamond among men—brawny and tough-looking but with a kindly heart. Since Tony was off duty and we had nothing better to do, the three of us got into a dice game. We rolled the bones on the porch floor, up against the side of the house. To begin with our bets were modest but as usually happens we got to doubling bets. First thing I knew, I had the dice and couldn't get rid of them. I either threw "snake eyes" or failed to make my point until I found myself one whole year's salary in the red and most of that pledged to my assistant. He wanted to quit while I was the big loser and he was the big winner. However, good old Tony said, "No, we'll stay here and shoot until Charlie is even or says he has had enough."

Well I sweated it out until I was only three months salary in debt and then quit. The next day I got an advance from the camp cashier and paid off my dice losses. I never rolled dice again for big money.

During the years 1912-1914, United States relations with Mexico waxed and waned. Possible invasion was a recurring specter to the Mexican politicos. Uncle Sam would woo the Federalists one day and the Rebels the next. As a matter of fact, the political scene changed so rapidly and so frequently in Mexico that even the citizens often were not sure which side they were on.

It was in this era that I was approached one day by John Armstrong to accompany the field superintendent (Mr. Dewey) and him on a mission for the U.S. Consul in Tuxpam to the Rebel headquarters in northern Veracruz on the Rio Tancochin near the Tamiahua lagoon. All three of us were Americans though we worked for a British oil company. Actually, I never knew the contents of the message—my part in the expedition was solely as a companion.

Our company put one of its fast little speed boats at our disposition and furnished a Mexican operator. We flew the

American flag as we sped over the waters toward the rendez-vous, feeling elated over the important assignment, but apprehensive at what might be our reception.

Toward dusk our boat rounded into the mouth of the Tancochin and proceeded up a narrowing channel flanked by high banks. We did not know the exact place where the Rebels were holding forth so we had to feel our way lest we overshoot the mark and maybe receive a salvo of bullets for our trouble.

Our boat was still going fairly fast as we rounded a big bend in the river, then—before we could stop the motor—a rifle shot whined across our bow. A Mexican soldier rode his horse down to the water's edge and shouted *Alto* as he drew down on us with his 30-30 rifle. We cut the motor but couldn't stop at once, and the speed boat kept sliding through the water away from the guard. The soldier rode along the bank parallel to us, with his rifle pointed at us, shouting, "Halt or I will shoot." He appeared drunk and certainly looked villainous. We were now almost nosed into the bank and could see the guard's finger dallying on the trigger. Needless to say, for a moment three Americans felt that they might be in for serious trouble.

For some reason or other the drunken guard did not shoot again. As soon as we had beached our craft, we identified ourselves as emissaries of the U.S. Consul, and asked to be taken to Colonel Aguilar at once. He seemed nonplussed but when we pointed to the American flag on our boat and emphasized that our business was official, he lowered his gun and staggered off to a nearby palm-thatched house. Soon other armed men appeared, who escorted us to the headquarters. There we presented our credentials and the sealed message, which the Colonel looked over with evident interest. After re-reading the message he smiled and offered us a drink and inquired about our trip, particularly if we had had any difficulty in finding his hide-out.

We told him all the details, including our reception by the drunken guard. Colonel Aguilar called in an orderly and said something relating to the guard, which I didn't hear. Later we learned that the guard had been shot the following morning.

Life was like that in those hectic days in Mexico.

It happened on January 28, 1914. I had left Tampico with an Englishman, an American lady and a Chinaman in the launch *Quest,* enroute for La Pena, a lake port on the Tamiahua Lagoon. We were more than halfway to our destination shortly after midday, when due to a south wind the lake became very rough. Our launch labored in the seas, rolling and tossing; however, the motor sounded good so we were not particularly concerned. Suddenly, while abreast of the north end of Isla del Toro, I saw a man in the water, swimming and calling for help. I stripped off my outer garments and pulled the fellow on board. As soon as he could get his breath he said that he was one of six men on board the launch *Tantoyuca* from Tuxpam, when it capsized about noon. We headed in the general direction of where the survivor thought his boat had gone down. Back and forth we cruised, around and around in large circles.

Our search paid off. Within a half hour we had pulled out of the water two other men and recovered the fourth (Lic. la Garza)* from the prow of the *Tantoyuca,* which had sunk stern first in about 15 feet of water. The last of the four was

---

*Lic. is the abbreviation for *Licenciado,* appellation of juri consults and commonly used instead of *Señor* when addressing lawyers.

taken on board about two o'clock, an hour and a half after the sinking. We cruised about for other possible survivors for another half hour before our low fuel supply forced us to abandon further search. Because of the rough seas and the elapsed time since the *Tantoyuca* had capsized, all the survivors agreed the other two men in their party must be presumed drowned—one of these was the owner of the boat.

While cruising about in the rough lake waters looking for those who had gone overboard, time and again our own craft nearly capsized. Our passengers were scared (and so was I). The Chinaman was down on his knees, the American lady cried and wrung her hands, while the Englishman just sat staring and held on for dear life.

On the way in, our motor began to give us trouble. First we had spark plug trouble then a little further on the gas line became clogged. Every time we stopped or slowed down for repairs our craft was tossed and buffeted by the wind and waves.

We finally limped into La Pena about 7:00 p.m.—hours late, but happy to arrive on firm ground again. The survivors were escorted to the local authorities, to report the accident and the drowning of two men, while the other Tampico passengers and I went on to Tanhuijo for the night.

The next day I returned to La Pena to see the authorities about the lagoon accident, but I did not go on to Tamiahua to report as suggested. Instead I sent a letter to Lic. Garza at Tamiahua where he had gone to report to the port authorities.

It developed that Lic. Garza was a rather well-known lawyer in Tuxpam. He appeared the part—well educated, well dressed, pleasant of face and speech. However, a few months later, I learned that Lic. Garza of Tuxpam was hanged by the military—whether by Federal or Rebel troops, I don't know.

There you have it. Saved from drowning to hang by the noose.

The American company with which I was associated bought a producing lease in the South Country from the Tepetate Petroleum Company. The agreement stipulated that the discovery well should produce on test for 10 consecutive days, 10,000 barrels a day of clean oil or no sale. Under the circumstances, all the Tepetate owners were on hand for the important test, including one of their larger stockholders from Pittsburgh. He was a nice, elderly gentleman but a rank tenderfoot to Mexico.

As we sat around camp waiting for the test, the old-timers began to tell stories of bandit trouble and the problems that arose when rival troops moved in and out of camp and sometimes used the camp as a battlefield. Normally, they said, if the invader came in the daytime, sober, there was nothing much to fear, but if a group of armed men came into camp at night, drunk, there would be trouble. We might need our side arms for protection if the invaders came in drunk, but if the invaders were sober, they would only take all saddlery, arms and ammunition in sight. So, it was always a question as to what to do when rumors were afloat that an armed group was headed our way. Should we hide our riding equipment and guns or keep them handy just in case they might be needed? As these stories went on and on, our guest became noticeably more and more concerned, much to the amusement of his hecklers.

One day a rumor came that a band of Rebel troops were in Los Naranjos camp, some fifteen miles to the south, and were moving in the direction of Tepetate. Every few hours a messenger would arrive in camp to say they were on the way or to announce that there was no sign of movement. We didn't know what or whom to believe. In the morning we would hide our saddles and guns in the monte but toward nightfall we would bring them back into camp to be handy in case the troops came inebriated. We did not all react the same—some were going to the monte with their belongings, while others were coming back with theirs. It was all very confusing. However, the VIP was most confused of all—he was practically worn out by dusk with his comings and goings.

After supper, the old-timers' tales got wilder and wilder. Finally, one of the fellows said, "I tell you what we'd best do, if we are to get any sleep at all, let's get ready for bed as we normally do. I'll stand guard and if I hear shots or the sound of advancing troops I'll awaken everyone and then we can all take to the monte."

"All right," said another old-timer, "but how will we know when it's all clear and safe to come back?"

"Very simple," said the first fellow, "I'll remain in camp and signal by whistling when the danger is over. In case you don't hear the all-clear whistle, you all shout from time to time and I will give the signal again." After some debate, the proposed plan was accepted without our VIP knowing that his leg was being pulled.

So, to bed we went, all except one of the chaps in the know, who slipped out into the night with his side arms. About an hour later several pistol shots were heard. Everyone scrambled into his clothes and grabbed his gun and valuables and beat it into the nearby woods. They went in all directions, to the four corners of the compass. Soon the old-timers began to drift back into camp, grinning. After a half hour or so all were safely inside except our VIP.

The night was quiet as far as human and animal sounds were concerned, but buzzing with awakened insect life. Now and then we heard the shouts of the VIP, first here and then there. No one made any reply. There were no more shots, no sound of troops—nothing save the buzz-buzz of mosquitoes, the chirp of crickets, the throaty croak of frogs and the now plaintive shouts of the very important person from Pittsburgh. By now he had been in the monte for some two hours. We began to be worried lest the ordeal be too much for his strength and heart. So we persuaded the initiator of the joke to sound the all-clear whistle and show a light. After a bit our friend came limping in, disheveled and covered with insect bites.

He asked where the troops were and, of course, we lied about the facts. They had been and gone, we said. No one told him differently for some days. When he found out he'd been hoaxed, he took it all with good grace, which made us feel ashamed for having played such a dirty trick on a very fine person—much older than any of us. But such was the extent to which men, living in those tense times in Mexico, would go to let off steam.

5

Geologist's Adventures

Hacienda Vinazco is located about 45 miles by river west of the Port of Tuxpam in Veracruz. The property consists of 5700 acres lying along the west bank of Rio de Vinazco, approximately 6 miles south of the Rio Tuxpam. This hacienda was purchased by a British oil company in May, 1912. That same year I graduated from the University of Oklahoma and was employed by the company. One of my first field assignments was to map the geology and topography of Vinazco.

From Tampico I got to my destination by launch through the Chijol Canal and Tamiahua Lagoon to Tanhuijo, thence by decauville railroad on a small 4-wheel dolly car drawn by two mules to Potrero del Llano and from there on horseback —three days en route. I had with me a letter of introduction (in Spanish) to the *Administrador,* a tall keen-eyed Mexican Indian, by the name of Gabino Obando. He put me up in the hacienda's main house which I made my field headquarters. A few hundred feet from the house, along the Camino Real, was the only cantina on the property—in fact it was the only bar and store for many miles around. The only people living on the property were the Indians who worked in the company fields and forest.

At that time I knew no Spanish and since no one on the property spoke any English I relied heavily on my *Lee and Laird Vest Pocket English-Spanish Dictionary*. However, the language problem was not too difficult, for the Spanish of the Mexican Indian is simple—mostly first person and present tense—and the Indians themselves were simple and kindly by nature.

One day when it was too wet for field work, I was seated with the Administrador on the wide porch of the house facing the Camino Real and the cantina. It happened to be a holiday and many of the local Indian men had come to the cantina for food and drink. Now, an Indian sober is a clean, decent, quiet, humble fellow, but an Indian drunk can be vicious and usually is unpredictable.

Along the east coast of Mexico, *aguardiente* is the peon's whiskey. It is raw cane alcohol, water white, and very potent. In the regions where sugar cane is grown, aguardiente is cheap, sometimes only a few centavos a tumbler. After a few drinks an Indian loses his inferiority complex, his inhibitions, his problems and feels released from the bondage which has shackled his race since the coming of the Conquistadores. The Mexican Indian drinks his aguardiente neat and in large gulps. The effect of this raw alcohol on the Indian is usually evident in three distinct stages: first, good fellowship, happiness and song; second, brawling, hatred and cursing; and finally, insensibility or stupor.

Knowing the frailties of his peons, Gabino Obando required all Indians trading at the company cantina to cache their knives, machetes and guns before the barkeeper would sell them any drinks. Such personal property was returned to the owner, when sober.

While I sat there some 30 or 40 Indians came to the cantina afoot and on horseback. These fellows were picturesque in their wide brim, conical-crown straw hats, their white cotton coat-shirts and white cotton pajama-like pants tied with cord around the ankle and their leather sandals; with their machete stuck through a colored sash around the waist and often a colored serape thrown over the shoulder. They were simple, healthy fellows, shouting and laughing like children. It was early afternoon. The day was warm. The rain had ceased and the sky had turned bright and clear. Only the wide Camino Real remained dark and muddy from the rains.

The Indians crowded into the cantina and were soon happy and singing. Suddenly there came a lull in the uproar and a few minutes later all hell broke loose. Men were cursing one another, their mothers, and their relatives, and fights broke out inside and outside the cantina. Soon it was a general free-for-all melee with fists, stones and clubs—each man against the other with no holds barred. They piled on each other and wrestled around in the muddy road. In a matter of minutes the picturesque, simple Indians had become ragged, muddy, drunken animals.

While this general brawl was going on in front of the cantina, one brawny disheveled young Indian approached the hacienda house—his face distorted in anger, muttering curses, with open knife in hand—and demanded that the Administrador come off the porch. I was scared but Obando seemed calm and cool. He arose and walked toward the half-crazed Indian, talking quietly all the while. I couldn't hear what was said but the drunken one appeared to relax somewhat and become less belligerent. Soon they were face to face. After a bit the peon put one arm around the Administrador's neck— the arm that held the open knife. Still Obando made no move except to drop his pistol hand onto the butt of his gun. Obando's back was toward me so I could plainly see the peon's knife as it passed to-and-fro across my friend's neck just touching the skin but not cutting. The Administrador's body was tense, but he made no move to thrust the fellow away—he just kept on talking. Minutes passed—it seemed like hours—before the Indian was pacified enough to drop his arm and reel away, back to the cantina. Whereupon Obando calmly walked back to the porch and sat down beside me. His only remark was that the barkeeper would be scolded for not disarming this young Indian before serving him. Apparently he felt no animosity toward the drunken one.

Once again we turned to the general melee. However, neither the Administrador nor his clerks made any move to interfere with the fighters or to stop the fracas. They just looked on quietly and expectantly. Naturally I was upset. As a tenderfoot American I was apprehensive that these Indians would not only hurt themselves but might even attack us. Finally I couldn't contain myself any longer and asked Obando if he wasn't going to do something to stop the battle royal. He replied that I needn't worry, they soon would fall unconscious from drink. I watched closely and, sure enough, in a little while the peons were collapsing wherever they stood —some in the mud of the road, one belly down across the fence and several on or half on their horses. The Administrador told me they would remain in that position until their drunk had worn off. The few Indians who had remained sober hauled their drunken friends out of the mud to the side of the road and off the horses to the ground. By then darkness was falling and lights began to flicker. All became quiet except for the snores of the drunks and the sounds of night life.

The next morning early, I arose and looked out to where the battle had held sway. All the drunken Indians of yesterday were gone—the cantina was deserted, inside and out. Normal hacienda life had been resumed—the holiday was over.

My assignment was to map the geology and topography of Vinazco. Usually I worked in the field with only one native to hold my rod while doing plane-table work or to cut trail through the brush and up along creeks while making compass and pace traverses. On Sundays and holidays my mozo had his time off and on those occasions I either stayed in camp to work up my notes or scouted the terrain alone.

On one of these no-helper days I decided to scout a nearby small stream in the hope of finding some outcropping country rock in the stream bed or along its banks, near the headwaters. Accordingly I set out alone, with my compass, notebook, pistol and a machete.

By noon I had worked my way up the little valley, mostly along the dry stream bed except where pools of deep water forced me to cut my trail through the vegetation along the banks. One water hole caused me to take to the bank amidst a *jimbal* (large clumps of giant bamboo) which stretched along both banks for some distance up and downstream. This jimbal was a huge mat of interlocking clumps of bamboo rising up twenty feet or more from the ground with butts or individual stems as much as six inches in diameter. This particular kind of giant bamboo had needle-sharp, strong barbs, shaped like a parrot's beak, along the stem. These barbs can do serious damage to flesh and clothing. Passage can be won only by cutting and slashing so I pulled out my machete and started cutting a path, slashing downward with the razor sharp blade, alternately right then left.

I had gotten well into the jimbal when suddenly I felt something soft, yet heavy, slithering down over the edge of my Stetson and onto my shoulder. I crouched, looked up and saw a large snake slipping tail first off its platform of matted bamboo leaves. Somehow I managed to back out from under that descending tail far enough to see that "my friend" was a young boa about eight feet long. Evidently I had jarred him off his sunny perch. Not caring to argue with such a formidable intruder and yet desiring to carry on my way, I dispatched him from this world with pistol and machete.

Although this boa was small as boas go (I've seen some in Mexico more than 20 feet long) it was big enough to have given me a big squeeze had it been able to coil around me. To put it mildly, having a large snake slither down over one's shoulder is a startling experience—especially when alone and deep in the jungle. Now and then I still dream of that boa.

Tucked way back from the river, in the hilly part of Vinazco, was a small village of Mexicana Indians. The Mexicanas are fine physical specimens—tall, strong and well-featured. Their homes are built of bamboo and palm, with well-swept dirt floors. The men dress in white cotton coat-shirts and white cotton drawerlike pants. The women wear brightly embroidered, sleeveless cotton blouses and full, short, home-spun cotton skirts embroidered with dyed wool yarn in an intricate colorful pattern. In coastal Mexico, each different Indian tribe has its own distinctive color and pattern design for their women's dress. Mexicanas generally are clean, simple and friendly in their villages. Since this particular village was located in a remote part of the hacienda, some distance from my base, I lived with these Indians for several days while geologizing in that area.

I ate their food, played with their babies and smoked with the men in the evening. We became good friends. Being unmarried and young at the time I had a roving eye for the women and I must admit that I liked what I saw—one young Indian girl especially. She was embroidering a new skirt, recently woven into a long narrow panel, the ends of which would eventually be sewed together and one side gathered in for the waist. She was making an interesting wide design of blue, black and red yarns for the hemline. It was a work of art—all homemade from local grown cotton fiber spun by hand into thread, then twisted into cord and finally warped on their own looms. The yarn came from Indian sheep and was locally dyed. The girl was attractive too—about seventeen, full-bosomed, strong limbed, and bronze-skinned. She was shy, but approachable in the presence of her own people. We made halting conversation about the skirt. She told me it was being made for the fiesta to be held that fall. I asked if she would sell it to me to take back to my sister in the United States. She protested that it was not yet completed and she couldn't possibly make another in time for the fiesta. I said her handiwork was lovely but even if she would not sell, would she consent to let me see the skirt when it was completed. She laughingly said she would, so the matter rested.

About two weeks later, after I had moved back to the hacienda house, word was brought to me from the village that the skirt was completed and I could see it if I still wanted to. I sent back word that I would be there the next day. Since my Indian friends had refused any payment for their hospitality while I was living with them, I got together a few rattles for the babies, trinkets for the women, cigarettes and cigars for the men and several cans of peaches as a treat for the whole family. My arrival was like a homecoming—all gathered around and accepted my small gifts with apparent sincere appreciation. There was much handshaking and many embrazos. "My girl" was there, resplendent in her new skirt. When the hubbub had settled down, I sought her out and again dickered to buy the skirt. Her parents abetted my case, until finally she relented and agreed to sell me her skirt for 15 pesos. When I accepted, she promptly unloosened the puckering string at the waist, let her new finery drop around her feet and scampered inside to put on her faded old skirt.

We still have that Indian skirt in our family, only it has been unsewn and is now used as a panel covering for the table.

Tamazunchale
(Pronounced "Thomas 'n Charlie")

From AAA: *Mexico by Motor* for 1957-1958:

Tamazunchale S.L.P. (pop. 5817, alt. 394 ft.). In the heart of the Huastican Indian country, Tamazunchale (Ta-ma-soon-chah'-leh) is an old and quaint tropical town. It lies on the south side of the Rio Moctezuma in the shadows of the Sierra Madre Oriental, the mountains which must be climbed before reaching Mexico's high central plateau. Now flourishing under the impetus of tourist travel, Tamazunchale was isolated from the outside world before the building of the Pan American Highway. . . . Valles, the nearest railway point, was 2 days distant by burro trail. Tamazunchale's sixteenth century church and its unusual Sunday market are of interest.

In 1913 my Mexican mozo and I rode into Tamazunchale which was then a small Indian village. We had no sooner appeared in the plaza in front of the old church than we were surrounded by a crowd of adults and children who followed us quietly to the local *cantina-tienda* where, we had been told in Valles, we might find a bed for the night. After dismounting and unloading my geologist's trappings my mozo took our animals off to the *potrero*.

The owner of the cantina was a Huasteca Indian who spoke some Spanish. I asked him why the crowds and why had they followed us across the plaza. I had difficulty understanding his mixture of Spanish idioms and Huastecan words; however, I gathered that the local Indians were having a religious fiesta and that I was the first American they had ever seen.

After removing the dust of our all-day ride, I strolled out into the plaza. The sound of weird music and chanting Indian voices had aroused my curiosity. A procession was passing—Indian priests, carrying a cross and a fearsome wooden statue of Christ, were followed by a straggling group of masked

Indian men and colorfully clad Indian women. It was apparent that the pageant comprised a mixture of Catholic and pagan rites. As soon as the priests had entered the incense-clouded church, the followers broke away and quickly surrounded me. The men had on papier-mache masks in the form of deer heads complete with horns, bull heads, bird heads and all sorts of headdresses—gaudy in life-like colors, with feather, ribbon and tinsel decorations. Each man held in one hand a painted wooden dagger with colored feathers around the handle, and in the other hand a carved gourd mounted on a short wooden handle. As the masked ones danced around me muttering an Indian chant, they shook their gourd rattles and made passes with their wooden daggers. I admit I was scared. Their chantlike cries became louder and their dance more furious. Obviously they were primitives, and I began to imagine all sorts of dire rites were to be my fate. Maybe, I thought, they were about to perform an ancient Aztec ceremony with me as the victim. Although armed with a Colt pistol, I realized I didn't have a chance with these hundreds of fanatics should a fight occur. When I tried to ease away, the milling crowd moved in closer. Finally I held up my arms in a surrender gesture and forced a laugh, whereupon others around me began to laugh too. Soon they were all shouting and giggling like children. The dancers stopped, drew off their masks and made friendly gestures. They made me understand by signs that they had never seen an American before and just wanted to have some fun.

I was so relieved to know I was not to be "sacrificed" that I made a liberal cash contribution to their *hicaras* (a half gourd bowl) and soon the crowd melted away to spend the gringo's money. However, before leaving, the head man of the funsters made me a present of a gourd rattle and a wooden dagger—which I still have.

The Huasteca Indians in the Tamazunchale area a half century ago were fine looking, tall, strong and bronze colored.

In the Sierras Oriental it was customary for the men to wear only breech clouts in summer and for the women to wear no clothing above the waist. However, during the regime of Profirio Diaz it was decreed that all Huasteca men must wear pantaloons and all women must have their breasts covered in public. That decree was in effect when I came to Tamazunchale. Soon, I noticed the Huastecas got around this clothing decree in an ingenious way. For example, the men would don pantaloons when they came into town to trade but would remove them when they left the village limits. I have seen several breech clouted Indians stop their burros short of town and pull a single pair of white cotton pantaloons (resembling underdrawers) out of their pack. These would be donned by one of the group who would then stride off to town to do his marketing. Upon his return the pants would be removed and passed on to the next man. To satsify the law and yet preserve freedom of movement, the Indian women devised a sort of napkin breastcloth with one corner tucked into the waistband in front and the other corner hanging loose to just below the shoulder blades at the back. The head projected through an off-center slit in the square white cloth. It answered the purpose, front-view, without binding like a blouse and without obstructing either side view or breeze.

As a young man I was impressed with these foothill Huasteca men and women, especially the latter. It seemed to me that they were magnificent physical specimens—sturdy, tall, erect and fine featured—like the Amazonians I'd read about. When on the trail the women would tuck up their normally knee length skirts into their waistbands, exposing their bronze thighs. As they strode up the steep paths of the hills, usually with a large basket of corn on their heads, their leg muscles would stand out like whipcords, only to melt into golden smoothness when they chanced to stop for a rest.

I am loath to return to Tamazunchale lest my memories be disillusioned. What was once a primitive Indian foothill village is now a bustling town on a great highway with gas stations, motels and tourist shops. I doubt if the Huasteca Indian maidens of today can be as impressive in beauty and stature as those of yesteryear.

On one assignment my assistant Burton Hartley and I went from northern Veracruz to the Isthmus of Tehuantepec to geologize some of the fee and leasehold properties of our company. Northern Veracruz is monte, rolling plains and bush country, while the Isthmus is jungle land, swamps and water. Not only is the landscape and vegetation different but there is a greater difference in the animal and bird life. Elsewhere in Mexico the traveler got from place to place overland by horse, carriage or foot, while in the Isthmus, except for the single railway crossing from the Gulf of Mexico to the Pacific Ocean, practically all travel was by boat.

For both of us the change in conditions was abrupt and created work and living problems we had not experienced before.

We arrived in Coatzacoalcos by steamer from Tampico and then proceeded to Minititlan where the company had its refinery and southern office. From Minititlan we traveled by launch about 30 miles up the Rios Coatzacoalcos and Uspanapa to a property called Filisola. It was this property that we were to survey, by canoe and on foot, with local Indian helpers.

The company held this property in fee. There were known oil seepages in the vicinity and several wells had been drilled on an adjoining property which were small producers of rather heavy oil. Upstream the Tecuanapa field was producing oil of good gravity. However, previous geologists who had examined Filisola's oil prospects gave negative reports. Our job was to re-examine and reappraise the property. On the basis of our findings the company would probably either sell or retain the hacienda.

Part of Filisola along the Rio Uspanapa had been cleared for raising bananas. Small ocean steamers drawing up to 18 feet could navigate the Uspanapa as far as Filisola, bringing dry cargo upstream from the United States and carrying away fruit. The only open trails on the property were in the banana plantation. In the cutting season a narrow gauge railway operated to carry the green bananas from field to dockside, where the bunches were corded like logwood. Incidentally, the crossties for this decauville railroad were solid mahogany and so were the frames of the little tram cars.

Two Scots ran the banana plantation, Mallison and Chinnery, representative-in-charge and general manager respectively. Chinnery had a Scotch lady housekeeper. All three were old-timers in the tropics, liked their whiskey in large doses, and were profane in speech but had hearts of gold. We were instructed to report to them and request their help in getting our survey under way.

Our first camp was set up on the river bank some miles upstream from the hacienda headquarters. We engaged local Indians with dugout canoes to transport our gear to camp site and to build our camp. These men quickly cut bamboo for the frame of a small two-room house, planted the corner posts in the ground, tied the bamboo uprights and cross members together with vines and then tied on palms over-all for the sides and roof. For coolness we stretched a tent fly over the house, leaving an air space between the canvas and the palm roof. Our helpers made for us split bamboo beds and tables and even improvised chairs out of bamboo and deer hides. Altogether, it was comfortable and perfectly adapted to the climate and conditions. In the background stood the house of one of our helpers (his young Indian wife agreed to act as our cook, do our laundry and mending), surrounded on three sides by giant tropical trees and a tangle of huge vines and creepers. In the foreground was the broad, deep Rio Uspanapa silently flowing toward the Gulf. The river was a wonderful highway for travel but not good for bathing—too many crocodiles.

Our first undertaking was to traverse the property's natural boundary, the river, after which we planned to cut our way inland. Except for the banana clearing, the hinterland was all jungle—giant hardwoods and tropical cedars, tall spindlly fern palms, great vines looping down, bamboo in profusion— so tall and dark the sun seldom got through the ceiling of leaves. Even when it was not raining the jungle dripped.

Everywhere were monkeys, rodents, birds of all kinds in their brilliant colors, and occasionally deer and wild hogs. There were numerous snakes and all manner of crawling things. It seemed to us this jungle was the Garden of Eden for all insect life. It literally swarmed with mosquitoes, gnats, flies and many other biting bugs, especially after nightfall. We wore fine mesh netting over our hats by day and slept under muslin netting at night. It was fever country.

We could make our way through the jungle only by hacking out a trail with machetes. In that damp, hot climate the trails had to be recut every three weeks or else they became obliterated by undergrowth.

Under such conditions we could not use the conventional methods of mapping but resorted to sketching cases and compass to orient our position and to make an approximate traverse. Nowadays an aerial photographic survey could make a better and more accurate map of this area in an hour than we could do afoot in two months. However, aerial photography cannot record the dip and strike of rocks concealed by jungle near the head waters of small tributary creeks. In that regard our foot traverse was justified.

The work was gruelling because of the heat and the harassing insects. Before we abandoned our first camp, Hartley came down with a severe case of malaria and had to go to the hospital at Minititlan. I carried on alone, save for my Indian boys.

My next camp was located on a little stream called the Santa Cruz which flowed out of a large swampy area into the Uspanapa. Before Hartley left, we had surmised this inland swamp might be the eroded crest of a large salt dome structure which I would try to prove or disprove by cutting a traverse all around the fringe of the swamp and running side traverses to the head waters of any stream that emptied into this swamp. My campaign was carried out as planned and the results indicated that the swamp area might be the crest of a large domelike structure. This "high" was afterwards drilled by my company. I was told that the drill entered rock salt some 700 feet below the surface but failed to find oil in commercial quantities.

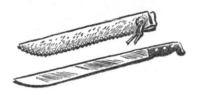

My favorite camp on Filisola was the one on the banks of the Santa Cruz. The camp site marked the limit of canoe navigation on the stream and also was the cross-roads of water travel and a dim, seldom-used overland trail between

Tecuanapa and Filisola. Except for one Indian family no one lived in the vicinity.

The Indian man was my mozo. His comely, shy, young wife was my cook and laundress, and their two little boys my buddies of an evening at the swimming hole. In addition the family included a nursing baby and an old grandmother. They were all clean, friendly folk, free with their simple kindness. I was able to reciprocate in part by offering them some tinned fruit and candy, but the thing they esteemed most was medicine. Grandma, particularly, suffered from her rheumatism and bad teeth. The former I could only alleviate temporarily with aspirin, but for her toothache I doled out chloroform paste to rub on her gums which afforded some relief. Grandma registered her keen appreciation by her wordless, almost toothless grin.

Although without any medical schooling, I had sold medical books one summer while I was in college. Having perused *The Favorite Medical Receipt Book and Home Doctor,* to effect better sales, I had absorbed some knowledge of the basic symptoms of common diseases and ailments. Because of that knowledge, such as it was, I carried with me a fair-sized kit of drugstore medicines, ointments and bandages, and a hypodermic outfit.

Evidently my prescriptions for their ailments and the fact that I had a medical kit gave these simple Indians an unwarranted faith and confidence in my medical ability. They called me their American doctor.

One evening, as I sat working on my notes under a mosquito bar in my little house, I became conscious of the prolonged distressed crying of a young baby. When my man brought in my supper I asked him what the trouble was. He said, "My baby is sick." He did not volunteer any more information, so I gave the matter little thought. The baby cried intermittently throughout the night and it was crying the next morning when we went out to work. It was still crying, a sort of moaning hungry cry, when we returned to camp late that afternoon. As soon as I had cleaned up, I called in the man and said, "Tell me more about your sick baby." He told me the mother had sore breasts and her milk had stopped, hence, the baby was hungry and would die unless they could get milk. I volunteered to look over the situation and together we went to his house. First I examined the baby which apparently had no fever or other symptoms of internal ailment—it just kept on crying, refusing any masticated food such as banana or tortillas. Obviously, the baby craved its normal diet of milk which was unavailable from the mother and there were no cows or goats in the area.

The young Indian mother and grandma were relieved to learn that the child was not sick but only hungry. I asked to see the mother's breast and without any false modesty she drew off her loose blouse, baring her upper body to the

waist. (Very unprofessionally no doubt, I could not help but mentally admire her golden torso and full breasts.) I felt of her breasts; both were stone hard, sore to touch and had a purplish hue. I remembered that my mother had had what our doctor called "caked breasts" while nursing my young sister, and I realized something must be done to relieve the congestion and restore normal blood circulation. With no breast pump handy, I figured the only hope of allaying the congestion in this case was massage, a penetrating ointment, and hot compresses.

I told grandma and the young mother of my diagnosis and suggested remedy but cautioned against having too much confidence in obtaining the desired relief. I told them that, if the mother's condition was not improved by morning, we would send the father to the nearest settlement in the hope of finding some condensed or powdered milk to save the baby. Both grandma and the young mother requested that I do whatever I could to relieve the mother's trouble.

Under my direction, grandma put a large vessel of water over the fire. Meanwhile I got from my duffle bag several yards of wide flannel bandage and a jar of Sharpsteen's ointment. (When my sister or I had chest colds mother used to grease us with this penetrating ointment, then cover our chests with brown paper and flannel cloth and finally, apply hot compresses—it gave us relief.) After grandma had placed several hot, wet cloths over the mother's breasts I rubbed the ointment in all around, over and under. Then more hot wet applications and another ointment massage. I counseled grandma to keep applying the hot compresses off and on all night and strode off to my bunk.

Again, the next morning I looked at my patient. Her breasts were now less hard and less sore to touch and had less of the bruised color appearance. With this encouragement, we postponed the canoe trip in search of tinned milk. Once again I massaged in the ointment and grandma applied the

hot, wet compresses. An older man, with professional training, might not have been as conscientious as I was about
massaging those breasts—but how was I, a young, unmarried
and medically untrained fellow, to know. Twice this operation
was performed before I left for work. Again, I counseled
grandma to keep applying the hot compresses.

That evening when the father and I returned from work
the first thing we noticed on entering the camp was silence,
no baby cries. We hurried to his home and met grandma
and mother, both smiling at the young baby contentedly
nursing at the mother's breast. The baby's life had been
saved. I cannot begin to describe their gratitude. It was
pathetic in simplicity and sincerity and moved me deeply.

Only a few days later these good Indian friends were able
to reciprocate by saving my life.

As mentioned, Tecuanapa lay up stream along the Rio
Uspanapa. It was an oil field of considerable importance in
those days, both for volume and high gravity production.
Consequently, that place was important in a military sense.
Whichever side, Rebel or Federal, held control of Tecuanapa
virtually controlled the indigenous supply of crude for the
Minititlan oil refinery.

Now, about the time of the caked-breast incident, there
had been a battle in and around Tecuanapa. We heard of
it by the grapevine but were not advised as to which side
won. However, I was not particularly worried about getting
mixed up in the fracas since my camp was isolated and lay
away from the main artery of travel, the river.

One night, about 2 a.m., my mozo (the father of the
baby) aroused me and said, "Jefe you must get up quickly,
pack all your things and let me take you by canoe down
river to the hacienda headquarters for safety."

"Juan, what's the trouble? How can we be in any danger
back here in the jungle?" I asked.

"Senor, I've just had word from an Indian friend who has made his way overland by the jungle trail tonight" said Juan. "A big battle has occurred at Tecuanapa and the losing forces are said to be headed overland this way with some wounded. Should they find you, an American, here they might take you captive or even kill you."

Knowing the danger of being come upon by a defeated band of soldiers, especially Rebels, I wasted no time in moving out as Juan had suggested.

We pushed off bag and baggage in the dark night leaving the women and children behind, as Juan assured me they were in no danger. Only a stranger was in danger, he said. We reached the Filisola banana plantation headquarters about daybreak where I was welcomed by Mallison and Chinnery and their housekeeper. They told me that it was the Federals who had won, not the Rebels. However, the Federals were evacuating their wounded and were expected to arrive shortly by launch and canoe down the big river. In the afternoon a band of soldiers, looking the worse for their rough fight in the monte, arrived with several wounded. Some of these poor fellows had laid out in the jungle bush for several days, too shot up to seek aid. One chap had received a bullet in his upper arm. Without treatment, his arm had swollen to the size of a man's thigh and the wound appeared infected. I tried to fix him up for the trip down stream to the hospital. First, I gave him an injection of morphine but, unfortunately for him, I stuck the needle in his arm below the wound instead of above the wound and closer to the heart. (This was the first and only hypo I ever endeavored to administer.) He protested that I hurt him when I probed for the bullet. I insisted he was a sissy—that after the hypo he couldn't possibly feel any pain. So while he squirmed and hollered, I poked and prodded. However, without proper instruments I could not find the lead in the angry looking wound. Obviously it was deep in that great mass of infected flesh. Finally, I gave up and washed the wound with bichloride of mercury solution and bandaged his arm. The soldier thanked me, but I didn't deserve any thanks for having given him such a needless bad time. Before night fell the soldiers took off for Minititlan by launch.

I stayed at the headquarters overnight, then went back to the jungle camp to complete my survey.

Later we found out that neither Federals nor Rebels had approached our camp, either overland or otherwise. So, as it turned out, I never was in any real danger. In my book, however, Juan saved my life by insisting that I vacate my camp for the safety of the plantation house and I expressed my heartfelt thanks to him and his family.

One week end after a long hot day in the field, I felt it advisable to go downstream to my base camp for more clothes and provisions. Afterward I asked one of my mozos (who had his family in the base camp) if he would take me back in his dugout canoe.

We started about dusk. Down the Santa Cruz we floated to its junction with the Rio Uspanapa, then out of that broad deep stream. The wind was blowing very hard, making small whitecaps on the river. As we paddled downstream, close to shore, I became apprehensive about the big bend where, most certainly, the water would be whipped by the wind into sizeable waves.

Now a wooden dugout, such as the Indians use in Tehuantepec, is long and large but very unstable. It can and does
roll over as easily as a log. Knowing that, and realizing that
it is difficult to control a canoe with only one paddler, I
became worried. To tip over in those shark and crocodile
infested waters could be serious. So I instructed my man to
put me ashore at my first camp site on Filisola where I knew
Juan and his wife would permit me to stay overnight.

As I clambered up the bank I called to my paddler sug-
gesting that he come also, but he said no, explaining that he
wanted to be with his family that night but would return for
me the next morning when the wind had died down. With
that he glided off rapidly downstream. It was not until the
canoe was out of hailing distance that I noted Juan's canoe
was not at the landing, but it did not register that Juan might
not be home.

I strode up to the house and helloed to Juan and Maria.
Maria came to the door, greeted me warmly and with true
Indian hospitality asked me to come in and sit. I entered
and threw my duffle bag in one corner before asking for
Juan. "But Senor," she said, "Juan is not here and will not
be home until tomorrow. He's gone down river to a village
to trade." (Well, there I was alone with a comely young Indian woman—high and dry for the night, as there was no
canoe and no foot trail to leave by.)

I apologized to Maria and explained my predicament. She
was not a bit nonplused. She said, "Senor you are always
welcome to spend the night in our home." "Somos amigos,"
she added with a sweet smile. Just then the baby began to
cry fretfully. Maria turned to the homemade cedar cradle
swinging on vines hung from the rafters, fussed over the baby
a moment and then turned to me and said, "Mi bebi es en-
fermo." "Yo lo creo el tiene virvuelo." (My baby is sick—I
think he has smallpox.) With that remark I strode over to the
cradle and looked down at the little brown naked mite. Sure

enough the baby's body was all covered with scabs and its head felt feverish.

Now what to do, I thought. If I stay the night I really will be exposed to smallpox. But I cannot weather the night in the jungle and cannot get away to another shelter, so stay I must.

Again I recalled *The Favorite Medical Receipt Book and Home Doctor,* which told what to do in emergencies such as this until the doctor comes. In this case no doctor was coming, but I must do everything and anything possible to protect Maria and me from contagion.

I opened my duffle bag and got out some potassium permanganate tablets and a can of carbolated vaseline. I washed my arms, hands, face and shoulders in the disinfectant, then greased the baby all over, from the top of its head to the soles of its feet. This was intended to soothe the itchy skin and to prevent, as far as possible, the escape of the flaking scabs. The application was at least successful in soothing the baby for it ceased crying. Then I turned my attention to Maria who was cook as well as mother. On my advice she washed her body with the disinfectant from the waist up, especially her breasts, hands and arms. That done, Maria nursed the baby and then washed in the disinfectant as before.

By this time night had fallen outside and the jungle came alive. Cat wheezes, the barks of monkeys, the sound of breaking brush as large animals came down to water, the twitter of birds and the ever increasing hum of insects became audible. Candles were lit and Maria busied herself before the open fire readying the evening meal of beans, chicken, tortillas and coffee. I sat in a homemade cedar-frame chair with a curved seat and back covered with deer hide—comfortably smoking my pipe but thinking of smallpox.

Smallpox is a dreadful scourge in the Isthmus country. Whole Indian villages are known to have been wiped out with plague. The Indian is a fatalist about smallpox—one either lives or dies. In his mind nothing can be done about this sickness except close all windows and doors to keep out the night air, and, if the patient dies, divide up his belongings among the relatives. Thus, the disease spreads and whole villages are decimated. To make matters worse, black smallpox is not unknown in the Isthmus. Black smallpox literally putrefies the body until the throat and lungs are affected, then the patient suffocates and dies—so I had been told.

I pondered my situation. Selfishly I thought more of myself than of either Maria or the baby. That Maria was desirable and might be willing never entered my mind. I was too concerned about smallpox.

After supper we again washed in disinfectant. I again greased the baby all over after which Maria nursed the infant. The baby had stopped its fretful crying and fell asleep.

Soon we were all asleep, though fitfully.

At daybreak, and again after breakfast, Maria and I bathed and I greased the baby. Obviously the child's fever had abated, and he was no longer irritable. An hour after sunup my mozo arrived from base camp with the canoe. Before saying good-by to Maria I left her a supply of the disinfectant and salve. There were tears in her eyes as we shook hands in farewell. As I walked away to the river bank, she called out, "Adios amigo, vaya con dios."

The river was quiet that day. The swift current aided by paddling quickly carried us to the base camp. There I arranged for a larger canoe with four paddlers to carry me down to Minititlan, and as soon as they had rigged a palm shelter amidships to ward off the sun and rain, we were off. All that day we traveled, reaching Minititlan in the shank of the evening. I paid off the men and headed straight for the hospital where I told my story. The doctors revaccinated me, gave me a purge and put me to bed.

I stuck around the town for several days but nothing happened. Finally, when I did not show any signs of having contracted smallpox, I returned to my field work.

Later I learned Maria's baby recovered with only a few minor pockmarks. Neither she nor Juan got the disease.

Throughout my stay on Filisola, Juan and Maria remained my very close and dear friends. Apparently they looked on me as a benefactor. Such were the ways of the simple, kindly, Indian folk on the Isthmus of Tehuantepec.

6

Exploration Hazards

In early February, 1913, eight months after coming to Mexico as a geologist for a British oil company, I was given the job of making a topographic and geologic survey of the Otontepec Mountains in northern Veracruz. Another geologist, fresh out of college, was assigned to assist me. Our entire party consisted of two young Americans, three Mexican mozos, five saddle horses and two pack mules. We carried no camping equipment as we planned to live off the country.

The Otontepecs are not a part of the Sierra Oriental but lie far to the east of those great folded rock masses. The Otontepecs rise boldly nearly 4,000 feet above the sea, towering, stark and black, over the rolling coastal plain—a huge island of basaltic intrusives. This geographic sentinel serves as monumental corner for the homelands of the Santa Maria Indians and several sub-divisions of the Huasteca Indians including the Tepezintlas, the Zacamixtles and the Tantocos. Because of superstition the Indians made little or no attempt to settle in the highlands, but located their principal villages and trading centers along the mountain trails which skirted around the base of the mountain mass. It was in these villages—Juan Felipe, Piedras Labrada, Tancoco, San Nicolas, Tamalin, Tantima, Citlaltepec, Chontla and Tepezintla —that we would successively base our operations as we moved counter clockwise around the mountains, traversing the basal trails and triangulating the more inaccessible high points inside the circle.

The mountain area was delightfully scenic. Its bald rocks, sharp ravines and rushing waters, its crisp cool air, its profusion of wild flowers and the bright flicker and song of birds was a marked contrast to the sultry lowlands lying on all sides.

Every weekday was market day in one of these villages. Traveling merchants moved from one town to another in rotation. Each of the villages specialized in certain homemade or homegrown merchandise. Tepezintla was famous for saddlery, Tancoco for straw sombreros, Zacamixtle for green groceries, Tantima for grains, Chontla for cattle and sheep and Citlaltepec for handloomed cloth. Each market day was a fiesta of sorts with food and drink being sold at improvised stalls, Indian musicians playing and singing, and cock fights and dancing as daily amusements. For the most part, merchants and customers were simple unspoiled Indians of the Otontepec Mountains. Their market day was always a colorful and happy occasion, in no sense commercialized for tourists.

Zacamixtle, our starting point, was the least interesting of any of the villages, being situated in a valley east of the main mountains on the edge of the oil country. Tantima and Chontla were trading centers for the contiguous lowlands to the north and west and as a consequence their peoples were a mixture of Spanish, Mexican and Indian without the character and virtue of any one of them. How-

ever, Citlaltepec, Tancoco and Tepezintla were pure Indian villages in speech, dress, custom and character. These
Indians were all clean living, simple, industrious, friendly
people, totally unspoiled by civilization, and virtually un-
changed since Cortez' time.

Of all these towns, I liked Citlaltepec (meaning, "place
of the stars") best. It stood on a rocky knife-like ridge,
high in the mountains. The bamboo houses, thatched with
palm, faced on the single street with their rear overhanging
steep slopes. The homes, their dirt floors swept clean, were
furnished only with cots, a chair or two, cedar tables, a
tiny altar on which candles burned day and night amidst
wild flowers, and a hand operated Singer sewing machine.
All cooking was done over an open fire in a smoke be-
grimed kitchen, but the food was always clean, well-sea-
soned and plentiful. The tortillas came off the griddle snow
white and piping hot, a gourmet's delight.

In Citlaltepec only the *jefe civil* spoke Spanish and it was
in his home that I lived for a week or more. Never have I
been treated more courteously anywhere by anybody. I was
given the best food and the best accommodations this Indian
family had, for which they would accept no payment in
money. On my departure I tried to show my appreciation
of their hospitality by giving presents to the family—candy
and toys to the children, bright colored ribbons and trinkets
to the women, cigars and liquor to the men and several cans
of California peaches for dessert at our last supper. We parted
the next morning with hearty embrazos and handshakes, dim
eyed, real friends.

All went well with our survey until we got to Chontla
(western gateway to the Santa Maria Ixcatepec Indian
country), the next to last base on our traverse. I had sent
a mozo ahead to locate sleeping quarters and an eating
place, as well as a potrero for our animals. The mozo reported Chontla had no hotel but he had arranged for my

assistant (Hartley) and me to bed down on cots in a new wing that had been built off from the pool and gaming room of the local cantina—we would dine elsewhere nearby. About dusk, when our day's work was done, we rode into Chontla. At the cantina our mozos carried the gear to our room while Hartley and I remained outside to instruct the boss mozo about caring for our horses and reporting to us the next morning. Our men finally moved off into the darkness with all our animals and saddlery.

Hartley and I entered the cantina to make for our room to freshen up before dinner. Soon as we had stuck our heads in the door we noted there were many men scattered around the pool room—some playing, some standing and others just sitting. When they saw that we were American there was dead silence for a minute and then mutterings. I could hear mumbled curses on all Americans generally and on certain engineers in particular. Something had happened—we didn't know what, but whatever it was our situation did not appear healthy. Hartley knew little or no Spanish and so did not understand the tense atmosphere. I stopped him from entering and said we had better forego washing up and proceed directly to supper in the hopes that matters would be resolved by bed time. So off we went to eat. About two hours later, failing to find our mozos who might have told us what was wrong with the world, we returned to the cantina. There we observed the crowd had increased to as many as forty men scattered around the pool room. We would have to cross this room to the far end to enter our bedroom, which had no exterior entrance.

A large round table had been drawn up in front of the door to our room, so close that we could not open the door without removing one or more chairs. Around this table sat four large brawny men—some of whom were evidently half drunk. The mutterings began again as we stepped inside only now the voices were even more hostile. "Muerte los Gringos" (kill the Americans) was shouted by many but they made no move toward us and no one pulled a gun. We had no-where to go but in; anyway, there was always the possibility that this whole affair was a joke of some kind. I cautioned Hartley to keep his arms close to his holster, but not to draw, and we moved in, saying in our best Spanish, "Buenos noches Senores," smiling friendly-like the while. No one drew a gun, although the shouts and curses became alarming. When I got to the table and made ready to set aside an empty chair blocking the door to our room, one of the biggest men around the table staggered to his feet, pulled a long knife from his belt and shouted, "Muerte los Gringos" and then added "Ustedes son Americanos, verdad?"

My holster was cut away at the bottom and top in such a way that I could shoot my 45 automatic pistol without

drawing. I dropped my hand over the pistol butt, raised the end toward my assailant's fat belly and said in Spanish —with shaking knees—"Yes, I am an American and what are you going to do about it." I realized that if my bluff didn't work it was good night for both Hartley and me. We might get several of them but we were too outnumbered to get away alive. There we stood, both breathing heavily, but ready for the first overt move of that raised knife.

After what seemed like minutes of tense staring one of the more sober men at the table rose and pulled the big fellow with the knife down into his chair, saying in Spanish, "Watch out or these Americans will kill you—besides we still don't know that they have invaded." This remark meant nothing to us at the time, but we dared not dally. With all the dignity and bravo we could muster we set a chair aside, quickly entered our room and slammed shut the heavy hardwood door. Outside there were loud shouts of "kill them" and a great banging on our door. We quietly laid out our guns, ammunition and knives on the cots, prepared to do battle to the bitter end. After about an hour of hectic tension, they moved away and by midnight all was quiet.

With the door locked and barricaded and with the only window tightly shuttered, we finally lay down to cat nap the rest of the night. The next morning we loaded our gear and rode off for the nearest oil camp at Potrero del Llano as fast as we could go. On arriving there late that afternoon we heard that President Madero and Vice President Suarez had been assassinated in the streets of Mexico City, and it was rumored throughout the country that the American army would invade. Apparently, that talk of invasion by a foreign force had aroused the half-caste Mexicans of Chontla, and Hartley and I were to have been the first Americans to die.

Needless to say we did not return to Chontla to finish our survey until all invasion talk had ceased. Even then we hastened our traverse to get out of the Santa Maria country as quickly as possible. We had no further trouble.

Altogether I spent some ten years in Mexico during the revolutionary days and World War I, but the Chontla incident was the only time I ever came near to drawing my gun.

On July 4, 1904, the first great gusher oil well in Mexico blew in wild. The blow came unexpectedly when the drill had reached a depth of about 1,800 feet and while the drilling crews were at lunch. There was no steel casing in the hole except for a few joints of surface pipe. The volcanic force of the suddenly released pressures belched up rock and fluid and opened up fissures in the ground all around the hole and underneath the steam boilers. Almost immediately the gas and oil exuding from the fissures caught fire, making it impossible for anyone to approach the well. Soon the hole began to crater—drilling rig, derrick, pumps and boilers, all disappeared. In spite of anything man could do an oil field was lost. Instead of another Spindletop there was only an ever enlarging crater spewing forth hot salt water, gobs of asphalt and sulphurous vapors to mark the site of the famous Dos Bocas discovery well.

This well marked the beginning of an extensive search for other oil fields south of Tampico in what later proved to be the fabulous "Golden Lane." It was the technique of those days in Mexico to drill with rotary tools down through the soft shale overburden and then to drill into the Tamasopa limestone with cable tools. During this drilling scramble, it was noted that there was a critical temperature zone at the oil-salt water contact. In one edge field it had been determined by temperature survey that crude oil in place had a temperature of 145° —150° Fahrenheit, while the underlying salt water was usually at least five degrees hotter. Because of this observed temperature differential, it became the practice of Lord Cowdrey's company to take temperature readings on all drilling wells as the tools reached the objective depth. This was done by lowering a battery of self-registering thermometers in a heavy metal tube lashed to the bailer. From experience it had been learned that one screw too many could mean a strong salt water flow instead of oil. Drillers were instructed to stop drilling whenever the temperature in the bottom of the hole suddenly jumped, and to produce whatever oil they then had.

Some eight years after Dos Bocas, I went to Mexico as a cub geologist for Lord Cowdrey's company. E. L. De-Golyer was my boss. No sooner had I parked my sheepskin in Tampico than I was sent down to the South Country to do some field work and to make temperature surveys on drilling wells. Notwithstanding the temperature records from drilling wells were significant, my boss felt they should be correlated to the fluid temperatures of the current Dos Bocas flow. So it happened that in 1913 I was assigned as a one-man party to observe Dos Bocas.

What had been started in 1904 as an eight-inch drilled hole into the underground was now a crater of some 40 acres in area. From this huge bowl an estimated 300,000 barrels of hot salt water was still pouring out daily through a creek into the Tamiahua Lagoon. I was both amazed and awed at what I saw. The potent hydrogen sulphide gas had killed everything. What had been lush monte was now a gaunt specter of dead trees. The air stunk with the smell of rotten eggs. There was no sign or sound of animal, bird or insect life. Nothing stirred in the breeze. The silence was appalling. It was eerie and frightening.

Since I was to work alone I had brought no camping equipment along but planned on putting up at one of the company's pipeline pump stations some miles away.

As soon as possible after arriving at this desolate spot, I walked all around the crater, as close to the edge as I dared go. From this survey I found that the great bowl had a high side flanked by a forest of dead trees and a low swampy side. Through this swamp poured the overflow of hot salt water, forming an oily stream without any vestige of either plant or fish life. Gingerly, I sampled the fluid temperature at a few places around the crater's edge and along the stream where the ground appeared firm enough to bear my weight. These surface-edge temperatures ranged upwards from 170° Fahrenheit. Obviously, the fluid must be even hotter with depth and away from the edge.

The entire surface of the dark fluid in the crater was in a constant motion of currents and eddies, whirlpools and blows of oily muck, hot salt water and evil smelling gas. It was evident that the high banks were undercut and could slough away into the heaving, seething, liquid cauldron. It was an awesome sight. It smelled and looked like I imagined hell might look and smell.

I wanted to devise a scheme to record the fluid temperatures near the crater center and to plumb the depths. However, I dared not venture forth in a boat because every now and then—without sound or tremor—the center would "boil" up 10 to 15 feet above the normal level and emit gobs of slimy, black oil and clouds of sulphurous steam. When these boils occurred, even when I was well back from the edge, I impulsively shrank further back. At the time there seemed to be no practical way of rigging a steel cable overhead from which a bosun chair could be suspended and moved at will across the crater. I concluded that my survey must be confined to recording a pattern of edge-surface temperatures all around the crater's perimeter. But even this presented serious risks to personal safety owing to crumbling banks on the high sides and soft muck on the low sides.

Finally, I decided on a fish pole device to throw my thermometers as far out into the crater as possible and yet recover them. I cut the largest and longest bamboo pole that I could handle and tied securely to the pole tip a long stout cord, on the opposite end of which I lashed a battery of three self-registering, metal encased, thermometers. With this rig I could stand back from the crater's edge, whip my bait well out into the cauldron and then reel in the record. After several days of scared effort, using the fish pole device, I had finished my assignment except for recording the fluid temperatures at the edge and surface below the high undercut banks. This promised to be the most risky of all the recordings but was necessary to complete the critical temperature pattern.

Thus came the final day—a bright warm Sunday—when, with mixed feelings of relief and dread, I went alone to that awful silent, dead woodland to make my last casts into the stinking, briny cauldron. Cautiously, I approached the edge of the crater and took a position near an old tree stump in order to have ample room for my long overhead cast. Twenty feet below, the oily, hot water swirled and eddied under the bank. When all set, I made a mighty heave that flung my heavy thermometers far out and down into the fluid inferno. Once the thermometers were in the fluid they must remain there for at least five minutes to ensure a positive reading. I braced myself and held my pole as steady as possible. The heat, the smell, the sight of hot, swirling water, and the lifeless surroundings were nauseating.

Suddenly, without warning, the very bank edge where I was perched gave way and slithered off. Instinctively, I reached up and groped with my hands as I slid downward. Fortunately, my hands struck a dead tree root, which the earth slide had uncovered. To this root I clung in desperation, first with one hand and then with both, my feet and body dangling over the evil hot water below. Unconsciously, I was praying that the root would hold and that I might be delivered from being boiled alive. I knew that if I fell, I must die and no one would know for days, if ever. Repeatedly I cried out for help but there was no one to hear. For two or three minutes I dangled over the cauldron before I could marshal enough strength to begin to slowly pull myself upward. Hand over hand I worked my way upward, fearing that the root would break. Dirt sifted into my eyes, sweat poured from my body, my head was splitting from the sulphur gas fumes and all my muscles ached from my dead weight and the tension of the situation. At long last I lay sprawled on the ground. Slowly, I inched along, away from the crater's edge to firm ground and there I lay face down and trembling all over, sobbing like a baby.

Never, in all my life, have I been so completely terrorized as at Dos Bocas, when I dangled over that seething crater of hot sulphur water—all alone—with only a root of a dead tree to save me from being boiled alive.

One of the great oil well gushers of all time was the famous Potrero del Llano No. 4 which blew in wild at 1911 feet in 1910. With the advent of World War I, when the Mexican revolution became rampant, the British owners of this well—then producing some 40,000 barrels daily—decided to erect a reinforced concrete bomb-proof shelter over the well connections as a protection against sabotage.

No. 4 was located on the edge of a broad shallow stream. During the many weeks this well was wild, oil had flooded the valley for a long stretch, especially after earthen dams were hastily thrown across the stream to impound the crude, which was then pumped out into huge earthen reservoirs. As a result of this flooding, the gravel beds all along the stream were saturated with oil, which solidified in the heat and air and became a natural wide-spread bed of impervious asphaltic gravel.

About a year after the bomb-proof shelter was erected, the gauges on the well connections showed a marked falling off in pressure and the tank gauges showed a falling off in daily production of oil. Coincidentally there occurred an outbreak of live oil and gas seepages which covered many acres around the massive concrete shelter.

This unheard of phenomena suggested either a fault or slippage in the underground beds or else that the casing had collapsed. The real trouble could not immediately be ascertained because of the erratic pattern of the seepages. It was suspected that the break lay below the asphalt beds and that the oil and gas probably had traveled some distance underground from the break before seeping up to the surface. There were over 130 groups of seepages, together producing nearly 2,000 barrels of 19° oil daily.

E. L. DeGolyer was then chief geologist for the Mexican Eagle Oil Company and was my boss. He had "discovered" Potrero del Llano No. 4. He thought that if we accurately mapped all these seepages and recorded the temperature of each exude we might discover a clue to the nature and location of the break. That was to be my job.

The mapping, done with plane table and telescopic alidade, was not a difficult job, though messy. Each seep, or group of seeps, was given a number and plotted to scale on the topographic plan. Taking the temperatures was more difficult and required placing a self-recording thermometer in each orifice and leaving it there long enough to obtain the actual temperature of the flow. While waiting for the thermometer to register, I made notes on estimated capacity of the particular seep in terms of barrels per day, the size and shape of the orifices, the estimated amount of gas accompanying the fluid, whether there was any sign of salt water with the oil, and other significant data. This work required me to have my nose close to the ground and seepages most of the day.

The oil pay in the Mexican wells of northern Veracruz was generally believed to be the Tamasopa limestone. This formation is exposed in the Sierra Oriental 100 miles or so west of the Golden Lane where it is dense massive, blue rock, seemingly impervious. However, underlying the prolific fields of the famous Golden Lane, the top of this oil reservoir rock was found to be full of oil-saturated pores and pugs, sometimes measuring inches across. It was theorized that this limestone had been subjected to the chemical action of circulating underground hot water which, over the ages, had leached out great pores and crevices in the otherwise massive hard rock. At any rate, the "pay" formation at Potrero was a highly porous limestone. The oil was hot when produced water-free, still hotter when produced with salt water, and always the associated gas was high in sulphur.

A mixture of H_2S with volatile hydrocarbons is wicked and very inflammable. One good whiff will cause a splitting headache. Breathing this gas for any considerable time would, and frequently did, knock a man cold. It was not a gas to fool with, especially as the use of gas masks was not common in the Mexican oil fields, back in 1914.

Day after day, I labored over my notes and thermometers—nose close to the fumes of hot oil and sulphur gas. My head ached constantly. Many times I felt "high." Once or twice I passed out and had to be resuscitated by my assistant. As the days passed, my headaches became extremely severe and my sight was affected. Both indications of gas poisoning worsened and then the glands all over my body got sore and swelled. Finally, as the job was about completed, I was invalided out of camp and back to Tampico. By that time I was so blind that I had to be led around. My condition was considered so grave that I was sent to the States for treatment and rest.

My assistant was able to finish our survey in short order while I was recuperating at home in Michigan. Fortunately, after a few weeks of hot and cold compresses on my eyes, good food, and a change of climate, all the symptoms faded, with no apparent bad effects.

Our mapping of the Potrero seeps proved to be conclusive in indicating that the oil seepages came from collapsed casing, rather than from any fracture of the underground. Eventually, the bomb shelter was removed with great difficulty and it was found that all the weight of this huge monolith had been hung onto the clamps around the top of the casing.* The sheer weight of the concrete mass had collapsed the casing string somewhere down the hole causing the oil to leak out into the surrounding formations beneath the "old blanket" of asphalt and gravel.

A concrete wall was erected around the well head, some

---

*This well had originally come in wild and was capped under the direction of Frank C. Laurie with a large leaded bell nipple tied down over the top of the casing with long heavy rods and giant clamps.

distance from the hole, and pumps were placed inside to remove the flow of seepage oil from within that area. A system
of concrete sumps and concrete-lined ditches were laid out to
catch and drain off the oil from the outlying seeps; there was
no way to control the escaping seepage gas. It was a serious
fire hazard. However, No. 4 continued to be produced in this
fashion until it caught fire during a hard electric storm. It
was a fiery furnace for weeks before being finally snuffed out.
That fire, and how it was brought under control, is another
story.

In Veracruz, lying between the foothills of the Sierra
Oriental on the west, the Cerro Otontepec on the east and
the Tuxpam River valley on the south, is the land of the Santa
Maria Indians. This tribe grew some crops, but for the most
part, they raised horses and cattle. Chontla, on the edge of the
Otontepec mountains, and Tantoyuca were their trading centers, being respectively on the east and west of their area.

The Santa Marias were cruel and undisciplined. They refused to let either Mexicans or foreigners cross their territory. Like the Seminoles of America, the Santa Marias were
never conquered, although they occasionally did service with
the armed forces. They were reportedly as bad and as *bravo*
as the Yaqui Indians. Their country was considered no man's
land by the traveler. Only well-armed large groups dared to
pass through.

Shortly after returning to Mexico in 1916 as chief geologist for an American oil company, I was assigned to look

over some properties on the west flank of the Santa Maria country. H. S. Walker, landman, E. W. Shaw and M. W. Clark, geologists, three Mexican mozos, and I rode our horses from Panuco to Tantoyuca — a hard two day's journey mostly through waterless, semi-desert country. On the trail we passed a wooden cross on which was perched a Stetson. Our guide told us that the cross marked the spot where young Daniels (said to be the nephew of Josephus Daniels, one time Secretary of the U. S. Navy) had been shot and killed by either bandits or Santa Maria Indians.

What had been broad camino reals in the days of Diaz and the Rurales were now but tracks through the bush. The villages along the trail had been moved inland away from the casual marauder. Thus, as we rode along single file, seeing and hearing no life except birds and animals, our coming on to this cross seemed a foreboding incident. We felt far from gay as we neared our destination about dusk.

We rode up to the best hotel in Tantoyuca and there unsaddled and stowed our gear in our one room which was equipped with four large canvas cots, four straight back chairs and one washstand with a single towel. While refreshing ourselves, we heard the sound of marching men in the street. We were told that this was a band of Federalists under General Melgosa (said to be a Santa Marian) passing through from the Santa Maria country to no-one-knew-where. All these soldiers were fierce looking and armed to the teeth.

Now Clark had complained of a bad tooth along the way and again on arrival. He said the pain was so bad he wasn't sure he could stand it without some relief. Since Tantoyuca had no dentists, Walker and I told Clark to apply hot compresses to his jaw in the hope that the inflammation would abate by morning. After supper we turned in, dead tired from our long ride. However, before midnight, Clark roused us and said he was going to start back to Panuco that night as his jaw was paining "something awful." Night travel in these parts was generally unhealthy because of mosquitoes and *tigreos* and was more so now that the contingent of Santa Marias was on the march. Clark however, maintained he had to go at once, so we located his mozo (an Indian boy by the name of Lucio Sanchez from Tempoal) who brought around their horses. Clark said he would skirt the Santa Maria country by traveling north to Tempoal and from there northeast to Panuco. If necessary, he would change horses in Tempoal at Senora Maria's, who had boarded our men and animals on previous visits. Our last words to Clark were, "Cuidado por los Santa Marias." Then Walker, Shaw and I went back to our cots.

The next morning, instead of heading east as we originally intended, the three of us rode in a southwesterly direction toward Platon Sanchez. At a ford of the river we stopped for lunch. As we sat there eating, Lucio rode up wild eyed, his horse all of a lather, and shouted that Clark had been captured by the Santa Maria soldiers. Lucio said he had dismounted and escaped into the night when the soldiers apprehended Clark, because he was afraid they would kill him for a spy. However, he had hung around the soldiers' camp for hours until Clark was finally released, stripped of clothes except for his underwear, and without his horse or gear. Together they made their way on foot to Senora Maria's, who got some clothes for Clark, fed them and outfitted them with horses and saddles. Clark had insisted on proceeding alone to Panuco but told Lucio to return to Tantoyuca and warn us of what had happened.

Instead of riding on into Platon Sanchez as planned, we rode along the west bank of the Tempoal River northward toward Tempoal—always on the *quien vive*. Several times that afternoon we met up with bands of Rebels who challenged us to halt and give what information we could regarding the whereabouts of the Federal troops. Being challenged by a mounted man holding a 30-30 rifle cocked and aimed at one's belly is nerve-racking to say the least—the gun barrel is usually only inches away from the belt buckle when the guard brings his mount to a rearing stop. Of course our pistols were concealed beneath our shirts on the inside of our waistbands; otherwise they would have been taken by the first group of Rebels.

We arrived at Tempoal about nightfall. Senora Maria completed Lucio's story. It seems that Clark, before being searched, had been able to conceal his pistol inside his underpants and throw away his holster. When the Indians went through all his belongings they found some extra pistol cartridges, his compass and notebook and promptly labeled him a spy. The angry soldiers clamored for his death but an officer prevented his summary execution. He was placed in a makeshift tent where he explained to the young officer who he was, his business, and why he was riding that night to Panuco. Apparently, the officer believed Clark's story and he suggested Clark escape as soon as possible. At first Clark was afraid that it was a trick—an excuse for the *ley del fuego* (law of escape, i.e. shoot to kill). The officer persisted, saying that if he did not escape soon the men would get out of hand and would surely kill and maybe torture him before morning. Clark finally became convinced and slipped away, almost naked, into the night where he was found by Lucio and put on the trail to Tempoal.

A few days later, after Walker, Shaw and I had completed our assignment, we headed our horses back to Panuco, from where we journeyed to Tampico by auto. The day after my return, Clark came to my office and asked permission to go home to Minnesota on a holiday. I knew he had gone through a harrowing experience so I consented to his leave. I was not really surprised when, some weeks later, I received a letter from Clark saying that out of deference to his parent's wishes he would not be returning to Mexico during these unsettled conditions.

On my recommendation, Clark was employed by my company in the mid-continent area of the United States. By the next year, field conditions in Mexico had improved so I sought him out when I was in the States and endeavored to persuade him to rejoin my force, saying that if all went well he would be considered for the chief geologist post. But Clark said no, explaining that now he had a girl and hoped to be married soon.

Clark remained in the law-abiding States only to be killed a few years later when his auto was hit by a train at a road crossing, in a pouring rain, somewhere in Southern Kansas. He had escaped from the wild Santa Maria soldiers in revolutionary Mexico to meet his death by accident in peaceful Kansas. Such is fate.

Strangely enough, my life was once saved by a Singer sewing machine in the heart of the Mexicana Indian country along the east coast of northern Veracruz.

It happened in 1916 shortly after I had been employed by an American oil company as chief geologist. At the time, my field staff had all resigned or gone on vacation due to the revolutionary conditions which were then at the worst. A cable had been received in our Tampico office, from New York, advising that the company had a thirty-day option to acquire an oil lease on the hacienda of Xuchil, which lay a considerable distance west of Potrero del Llano. Now thirty days is a short period for any sort of geological survey of readily accessible property but far too short a period to make a comprehensive examination of a remote area deep in Mexicana Indian country. Under the circumstances, I must do the reconnaissance myself with the minimum of assistance and outfit for mobility and speed.

I chose Ernest Hallett, one of our landmen, to accompany me. Hallett was an Englishman who had lived in Mexico for many years and spoke Spanish fluently. Together we drove by auto from Tampico to Panuco where we obtained two sturdy horses for our long ride into the hinterland. Each of us carried saddle bags with a change of underwear, an extra shirt, extra socks, a light blanket, rain poncho, a toilet kit and a few tins of sweets. Since our route would take us in and out of Rebel and Federal country several times, we dispensed with our usual heavy side arms and took only 25 calibre pistols which we carried in shoulder holsters beneath our shirts. We knew from experience that guns of any sort are favorite loot for marauders—hence, the probability of getting through with either rifle or side arms was most unlikely. We both carried saddle machetes, not for defense but for cutting trails.

The next day Hallett and I rode from Panuco to Tempoal, where we picked up an Indian guide-mozo by the name of Lucio Blanco, whom I had previously used when working in that area.

We planned our route to avoid the Santa Maria Indians and rode out of Tempoal directly south to Platon Sanchez instead of taking the better traveled trail to Tantoyuca. As expected, we met up with some roving Rebels. However, they were sober and we easily talked them out of molesting us and from taking any of our animals or outfit.

After spending the night in Platon Sanchez, we moved on southwestward to Chicontepec in the foothills of the Sierra Oriental. On the way, Lucio's horse became so lame that it was obvious we would have to leave it behind. We found that another animal was hard to come by in Chicontepec as the town had been recently visited by troops who commandeered all serviceable horses and mules. However, the soldiers had passed up an old white Missouri mule, which, we were told, had been imported by one of the oil companies several years ago, when many earthen reservoirs were built to hold the oil escaping from wild wells. Our purchase was a huge rawboned animal and would move only at a snail's pace, but it moved. This mule was the cause of serious trouble for Lucio later on in our journey.

According to our maps Xuchil was only about 10 miles due east of Chicontepec along the camino real to Tuxpam. In the days of Porfirio Diaz, a system of camino reals had been laid out all over the country. They were, in fact, natural trails from one settlement to another, broadened and maintained by the respective land owners through whose property they passed. Every land owner was required to render certain man-days a year to road maintenance. These caminos were neither graded nor drained, but when the monte was cut back and weeds and scrubs cleared away, the sun kept these broad trails passable most of the year. However, since the revolution began, there had been no road maintenance in this part of rural Mexico, and villages, which formerly lay along the main arteries of travel, had been removed into the monte. Many of the landmarks of yesterday had been obliterated from trail side and the roads were now only narrow, muddy paths through the undergrowth. Our problem of finding Xuchil was further complicated by the fact that no one in our three-man party had ever visited Xuchil before.

After a two-day stopover in Chicontepec, we got on our way shortly after noon. It was slow going. The trail was always either rocky or sloppy. Now and then, Hallet and I had to halt our mounts and wait for Lucio's slow-moving mule to catch up. We passed no signs of settlements and no travelers. Literally we were headed into the unknown. Hour after hour we plodded along through the heat of the day and on into the late afternoon. According to our reckoning we should have long since neared Xuchil but still there was no sign of habitation. We were getting anxious. Somewhere ahead was the Santa Maria Indian country where travelers were known to have been tortured and killed without provocation. Unless we sighted Xuchil soon we would be forced to sleep in the insect-infested monte since we had come too far from Chicontepec to be able to find our way back there after nightfall. Just as we were about to give up, Lucio spied smoke rising from the trees some distance back from the trail. As dusk fell we rode into a clearing around which were five or six bamboo-sided palm-thatched houses and *galeros**. On inquiry, we found that we had indeed arrived at Xuchil.

The natives in the area of Xuchil are Mexicanas—tall, swarthy and rather hostile in appearance. I believe it was the custom to bind the babies' heads; at any rate, the heads of these adult Indians were somewhat conical and sloped back from the forehead. The men, especially, were fierce looking with heavy black hair growing almost down to their bushy brows from which glowered piercing black eyes. All the inhabitants of Xuchil were Indians and only the Administrador spoke fluent Spanish.

When we rode up there were no men in sight. We called to one of the women and asked for the Administrador by name. By signs, she made us understand he was out in

*A galero is an open sided, palm roofed shed with dirt floor, used like a porch but not attached to a house.

the field with the other men but would return shortly. There was nothing to do but wait, so we sat on log benches in the shade of the principal galero.

Finally, just about dark, the men came in. The Administrador and his two brothers approached us—huge, powerful, fierce looking men, swinging their large field machetes. I promptly showed the Administrador the cable I had received from New York. Unfortunately it was in English, so my explanation fell on deaf ears. I produced my Spanish calling card, showing my name, my company's name and my profession (Ingeniero Geologo) and said our reconnaissance of his hacienda would only take a few days. The Administrador and his brothers stood and stared. They talked together in Mexicana, a language which neither Hallet nor I understood. Finally, the boss man said he would not permit us to survey Xuchil since he had received no direct word from the owner. Hallet and I both argued that we had ridden far to do what his owner had authorized and that our work would harm nobody or molest anything. Again the answer was, "No." When we asked if we could at least pass the night there, the Administrador protested they had neither food nor beds for our party. The attitude of the Administrador and his brothers had become increasingly adamant and belligerent. We were completely nonplused—what could we do, where could we go? I consulted Hallett in English. We agreed there was no way out but to sit and hope for the best.

So Hallett and I sat down on one of the log benches facing the Administrador's house less than five yards away. Both of us folded our arms in such a way that we could, if necessary, pull and fire our pistols without difficulty. No sooner had we seated ourselves than the three big Indians pulled up a bench alongside of the house and sat down facing us. Then, muttering among themselves in Mexicana, staring at us the while, each placed a flat piece of sandstone on his knee and began to sharpen his machete. Whet-whet, stare-

stare, whet—stare—whet! The suspense was awful. Hallett had a nervous affliction of twitching his head and neck—it seemed like his head was going to fly off with his jerkings. We were both sweating profusely. No one spoke. There was just the sound of steel on stone and the heavy breathing of angry men. Minutes passed. Death seemed to be breathing down our necks.

I was saying to myself, it can happen any moment now, when from across the clearing an old Indian woman hurried up to the Administrador. (I believe it was his mother, but I never knew for certain.) They whispered back and forth until finally he laid down his machete, removed the whetstone from his lap and stood up, still staring. Then in Spanish he said, "Senor, you say you are an engineer?"

I said, "Yes, I am an Engineer-Geologist."

"Then if that is so," replied the Administrador, "you fix this old woman's machine—follow her."

I turned to Hallett and told him to stay "as is" while I went to see what machine they were talking about, and added, "May God help me to fix it." Hallett nodded that he understood. I arose and followed the old woman to a bamboo-thatched house which had two dirt floored rooms and a kitchen lean-to. In the first room were a few pieces of handmade cedar furniture and a couple of canvas cots. Several oldsters and some children were gathered inside. The old woman said something in Mexicana and made signs for me to follow her into the next room. There stood a hand operated Singer sewing machine on a wooden table, with a deer hide chair drawn up in front—no other furniture, nothing. The old woman made me understand by signs that this was the machine which I, being an engineer, was to fix.

I sat down and asked for candles since it was by now almost dark. Candles were brought and lighted. I solemnly looked the ancient machine over very carefully, then made signs that I wanted some cloth to try in the machine. When I tried sewing the bottom thread broke. I re-threaded and tried again with the same result. I checked the bobbin and saw it was full. (When a young boy, I used to watch my mother at her sewing machine and had observed her wind the bobbin, adjust screws, rethread and sew. What did she do when one of the threads broke—I tried to remember—could it be that somewhere or other there was a tension screw out of adjustment? Such were the thoughts that flashed through my mind in this gloomy Indian house.) Maybe a tension screw was out of adjust-ment, but where was it located and how was I to know when it had been properly adjusted?

I pulled out my pocket knife and tinkered with this and that. With my fingers I turned and twisted everything on the machine that would move. Finally, I got it but in-stead of letting on immediately, I solemnly tinkered and went into a deep study. Finally, I insisted on having a new piece of cloth, something never worn or washed. After a lot of talking and running about from house to house the old woman came back with a bit of white cotton home-spun. Carefully, I rechecked the bobbin and threaded the needle, laid the cloth under the needle, lowered the foot and started cranking the handle. Back and forth I ran the cloth. The stitches were holding—the machine was fixed. With a dramatic gesture I pulled out the cloth, cut the thread and held it up for all to see. There were exclama-tions of mingled delight and awe from the women and children around me. The old woman beamed as she said in halting Spanish, "Mucha gracias, Senor, cuanto debe usted?" (Many thanks, Sir—how much do I owe you?) I arose, smiled and bowing slightly, replied, "You owe me nothing. I am happy to be of service to my friends." With that I stalked out into the night and back to Hallett under the galero.

I had no sooner told Hallett of what had occurred than the old woman was buzzing the news in the Administrador's ear (as I had expected). The three men got up and went inside the house. After a few minutes the boss man came out and smiled at us for the first time. He offered his apology for not having food and lodging of the sort Americans are accustomed to, but he would give us the best they had if we wanted to stay overnight. Naturally, we were relieved that the crisis was over, at least for the night, so we accepted whatever their hospitality could afford.

It was not long before a table was brought out under the galero, on which were placed homemade clay platters of *tortillas, frijoles, huevos fritos, pollo, chiles jalapenos,* and *queso,* followed by cups of hot black coffee. It was a feast for the gods—especially for two tired, hungry and recently scared extranjeros. After our supper, the men joined us for a smoke. One brought out a small guitar and began to sing native songs. Hallett told some off-color stories in Spanish which caused the Administrador to laugh—he translated for his brothers and they laughed, too. I clog danced and did a simple sleight of hand trick which seemed to go over in a big way. Soon all was gaiety where it had been gloom.

When it came time to turn in, the Administrador said he was most sorry, but they had only one cot for the two of us, and we would have to make-shift under the galero. We thanked him and assured him we would be happy with one cot, out under the galero. Hallett and I drew lots for the cot. I won, so Hallett lay down on the log bench. We didn't sleep well for nightmares, mosquitoes and the pigs. The pigs kept rubbing their backs on the underside of my canvas cot and scratching their sides on the bottoms of Hallett's feet. It was a grand night for sleeping, but not for us. Once Hallett jerked so hard in his sleep that he fell off his narrow bench and came up shouting and tugging at his pistol. He had dreamed we were being attacked. Fortunately, we both awakened before he started shooting or there might have been real trouble.

The next day the Administrador consented to my making a hurried geological examination of the Xuchil property. Never before or since have I covered so much ground in so little time. Nowhere on the property did I find any signs of oil or gas or any significant exposures of sedimentary rocks. In less than a day I had all the information I needed to render a "no lease" report.

The next day we parted with our new friends. Instead of going back by way of Chicontepec we decided on going east through the Santa Maria Indian country to Aragon and Potrero del Llano. It was on the return trip that Lucio almost lost his life because of his Missouri mule.

After my hurried geological examination of the petroleum prospects of Xuchil, Hallett, Lucio and I were returning to Veracruz by way of the oil camps to the east. Outbound we had come in from the north and west and had encountered en route a number of roving armed bands. So instead of retracking, we decided to proceed east through the Santa Maria Indian country to Aragon and thence, to the nearest oil camp at Potrero del Llano. We were partially influenced in this decision by the knowledge that our mozo's Missouri mule was so dead beat it could not be expected to stay on its feet all the way back to Tempoal, our mozo's home town.

According to our maps, the trail to Potrero from Xuchil was much shorter than to Tempoal. Furthermore the Administrador of Xuchil offered to send one of his boys along on foot to guide us safely through the Santa Marias.

This matter of a guide was the deciding factor. We had been told in Chicontepec that no traveler had passed through the Santa Maria Indian country and lived to tell of it, for the last three months. It would be too risky to attempt except with someone the Santa Maria outposts knew and trusted. Our Xuchil friends assured us that with their guide we could come to no harm.

It was mid-morning when Hallett and I bade farewell to Xuchil and the old woman who had asked me to repair her sewing machine. We were leaving good friends with considerable regret. Unarmed, except for the small pistols under our shirts and light saddle machetes, the three of us mounted our animals and, with our guide on foot, set forth to cross the Santa Maria Indian country which snuggled up to the east border of the hacienda Xuchil. The Administrador had told us our trail would lie through "forbidden land" for a distance of some 12 miles—five to six hours of hard riding—and that we would see no visible signs of habitation anywhere along this entire stretch.

Our Xuchil friend was so right. Mile after mile we plodded along behind our Indian guide. We saw no sign of human life and heard nothing except bird song and the occasional rustle of a wild animal in the bush. Our guide spoke no Spanish but he made us understand that certain bird calls were signals of the Santa Marias. Each time we heard those calls our boy would stop and reply in kind. Then, he would wait for the answering whistle (probably the "all clear—proceed") before striding on. Every time the guide stopped, we stopped, too. One time there was such an outbreak of calls from both sides of the trail and such a long wait before our guide moved forward again that Hallett and I exchanged meaningful glances—this is it, we thought. It was past mid-day when our guide finally halted and made signs telling us that we were now out of danger from the Santa Marias and that he was going back to Xuchil. We rewarded him with money and cigars, bade him Godspeed and he was off on the return trek.

Now we were on our own and, incidentally, lost. We were making for an Indian community property known as Aragon in the fertile valley of Rio Aragon. It had been at one time a large hacienda with one owner but in recent years it had been divided into 10 or 20 hectare* lots and sold to the Indians for farms. The main village of Aragon was shown on our maps to be located on the camino real, only a short ride from where we were when our Xuchil guide turned back. But, in the several years which had elapsed since I was last in this area, the broad, clear, camino real had become a narrow trail through the dark monte. Although we kept riding eastward I did not recognize a single landmark. There were no villages or any habitation along our trail. We saw no one. Neither Hallett nor Lucio had ever been in these parts before, so they looked to me to find the way. The sun was beginning to set before I realized that we must have passed Aragon along the way, although none of us had noticed any side trails. I knew our trail would eventually bring us out to the Tuxpam River but I also knew that we could not possibly reach Tuxpam until after midnight at our rate of travel.

Just as we were about to halt and prepare for a night in the woods, we heard sounds of approaching horsemen. With some trepidation we rode on—they might be fellow travelers or they might be soldiers or bandits. When we came abreast in the near darkness we saw several Mexican men and women with their mozos, all armed to the teeth with rifles, pistols and knives. We gave them a hearty, "Buenos tardes, amigos," to

---

*A hectare is about 2½ acres.

which they made a meager reply. We halted and asked them if they could tell us how to get to Aragon. They kept moving away and only called back, "No." We were nonplused over their attitude, so unlike the cordial treatment usually accorded fellow travelers on the trail in Mexico.

As we rode on it suddenly occurred to me that our best bet was to turn and follow the party that had just passed us. At this time of night such a mixed party must be going to some nearby habitation. Hallett concurred. So as quietly as possible, we turned and followed the sound of the party, keeping out of sight. After about an hour of such blind riding we lost the sound of the party. Evidently they had turned off the main trail or were lying in wait for us. Cautiously we advanced. After considerable searching we found the tracks of horses headed into the monte on the faintest of paths. We turned off into the woods and urged our animals on as fast as they would go. We wanted to get within hearing distance of the other party lest we become completely lost in this tangle of brush, trees and vines. However, before we sighted the other travelers we saw the lights of a village. We rode on into the clearing, unchallenged, and inquired of the first people we saw if this was Aragon. When our informants said it was, I asked for Senor Mendez, the head man, for whom I had a letter, and was told where he lived. We rode across the commons to Senor Mendez' house and I delivered my letter to him personally. He read the note and graciously said we could talk about a possible oil lease the next day, meanwhile we were to be his guests. After a very trying and tiresome day, all three of us were happy to find an overnight haven among friendly Indians.

We spent the night in the grainery in the loft of our host's home. For beds, we slept very comfortably on a pile of sweet smelling dry corn husks.

Early next morning I discussed the oil lease question with Senor Mendez and quickly came to terms. That done, I told our host we would like to press on to Potrero and inquired about which troops were holding what. I knew Potrero del Llano was the headquarters for General Manuel Palaez of the Rebel forces. The Rebels now controlled all of the South Country oil fields, and I assumed the Federalists would be holding the outlying territory. Senor Mendez confirmed my understanding of the situation and said there was, in fact, a Federalist camp a few hours journey from Aragon, along the trail to Potrero. He offered to send along a guide to take us to that camp and see us through the lines. We accepted and were soon on our way.

Shortly after noon we came in sight of troops and light field gun emplacements on top of a rise of open ground along our road. We were passed by the guard after he had challenged us and questioned our Aragon guide. The guide turned back and we pressed on alone. Hallett and I agreed that this cavalry force must be well mounted and formidable. Being in more open country where the trail was wide and clear, we urged our tired animals into a trot. Lucio and his old wornout mule were soon left behind.

About five o'clock we encountered the Rebel outposts where we were challenged by the guard and interrogated by officers. Who were we—whom did we work for—where had we come from—had we seen any Federals along the way—how many Federals—and where were they? We replied frankly and to the best of our knowledge. We were finally passed through the lines and made our way into the British oil company's camp. There I told the superintendent our story and asked that I be informed when Lucio arrived.

Our welcome in the Potrero camp was warm and genuine. Both Hallett and I had previously worked for this company and we found many good friends and former associates in the mess hall and at the club. We felt quite relaxed now that the most arduous and hazardous part of our trip was over. We had a pleasant evening reminiscing with the other old-timers.

Our conversation ran the gamut of wine, women, oil business, revolution and politics—past, present and future.

Just before we turned into our bunks, I inquired at the office and found that they had had no word of Lucio. Naturally, we were worried but there was nothing we could do, for we had no idea where he might be. So we lay down to sleep. However, shortly after midnight a messenger awakened me to say that Lucio was in the Rebel guardhouse, accused of being a Federalist spy, and would probably be shot in the morning unless we intervened. Hallett and I hastily dressed and made our way to the guardhouse where we talked to a young Mexican officer. He explained that several hours ago Lucio had arrived at their outpost on foot leading an old white Missouri mule. He said Lucio had denied seeing any Federals along the way and claimed he had recently bought the mule in Chicontepec—"Obviously the man is lying," said the officer. "No one dares cross through the Santa Maria country except with a strong armed force—furthermore, he claimed Tempoal as his home and everyone knows Tempoal is in Federal territory." As we listened we began to comprehend that our timid but loyal Lucio had not told the guard that he was our mozo and probably had not dared make an observation about the nearby Federal troops, not knowing what we had reported, for fear of implicating us. At once we told our story in all its details to the officer of the guard. Then, together we confronted Lucio who admitted his hesitancy about telling the Rebels he was our mozo and about making any comment about the Federals lest he involve *mi jefes* (Hallett and me).

The officer seemed convinced but hesitated to release Lucio until he had reported to the officer in charge next morning. Meanwhile he assured us Lucio would not be harmed. Hallett slipped the officer several hundred pesos to compensate him for his time, trouble and understanding. After bidding Lucio a good night we went back to Potrero.

Lucio was released to us early the next day. He was almost all in from fatigue and fright, so I was not surprised when he requested permission to leave us at Potrero and proceed to his home. Going by way of the pipeline route to Horconcitas, thence, across country through Ozuluama to Tempoal he would cross the lines (from Rebel to Federal) only once, somewhere west of the Horconcitas pump station. Since Hallett and I desired to remain in the oil camps several days and then return to Tampico by auto or launch, we readily acquiesced to Lucio's request. However, we suggested that he lead our saddle horses to Horconcitas and leave them there in the corral until we sent for them. He seemed entirely happy with this arrangement.

Eventually, we got back to Tampico and learned that Lucio had passed through Horconcitas and left our animals. I believe he arrived safely in Tempoal, although I never saw him again. Lucio Blanco, Indian boy, was the best and most faithful mozo I ever had.

7

Some Vignettes of Jungle Life

The junglelands of the Isthmus de Tehuantepec
teem with all kinds of wild life. During the day bands
of small monkeys rush about chattering, birds of brilliant
plumage flash through the bush and tall trees, snakes slither
across the trails, lizards scamper here and there, wild hogs
and peccary rustle and grunt under the sapote trees as they
search for fallen fruit, now and then a deer bounds past,
while around the swamps may be seen numerous crocodiles,
occasionally a tapir, and vast flocks of water birds. The night
is alive with the hum and buzz of insects, the barklike call
of the great monkeys, the cry of big cats and the crash of
large animals moving through the undergrowth.

Nobody attempts to traverse the jungle at night, except the
fugitive or hunter — it is not safe. However, travel by day
along an open trail can be a constantly changing picture of
color, sun and shadow, fluttering ferns and leaves, flashing

birds and butterflies, crawling things, moving animals and a myriad of odors. Obviously, even the day traveler feels more secure in his strange surroundings if armed with gun and knife.

Such was the hinterland of Filisola, away from the Rio Uspanapa. That was the jungle area where I was to make a geological survey afoot. Daily, throughout my exploration one or more Indian mozos preceded me, cutting trail through the tangle of thorny brush and great looping vines.

Each morning I left camp loaded down with instruments, lunch, canteen, side arms and machete. I wore a cotton shirt, riding breeches, knee boots and a stiff brim hat covered with a fine mesh netting which hung down over the shoulders. Usually, the underbrush was wet with dew or rain when we went forth and, what with the dripping jungle, the frequent rain showers, and perspiration I was drenched all day long, every day of field work.

It was so sultry that the human body required more than the normal intake of water. My machete men sweated as much as I did yet they never carried drinking water and never drank from standing water. I wondered how they managed until one day, when I had emptied my canteen by midafternoon and my tongue was practically hanging out, one of my Indian helpers asked if I would like a drink of cool, pure water. Naturally I said that I would. No sooner had I spoken than he walked over to a big looping vine, machete in hand. The vine was about five inches in diameter at the bottom of the loop, which did not quite touch the ground, and the ends were out of sight in the tall trees. With one slash of the knife the vine was severed just above the bottom of the loop. Then the Indian lad lifted one end of the severed vine and whacked off a piece about thirty inches long which he quickly handed me and motioned me to hold it up above my head at an angle, allowing the lower end to touch my open mouth. I did as directed and out flowed more than a quart of clear, cool water. I never had a more satisfying drink. After that experience I never again carried a canteen while at work in the jungle. The supply of these great looped vines seemed inexhaustible and served to supplement running water which we frequently found.

My native boys shifted for themselves for food and lodging. From their homes in the vicinity, they brought wool ponchos which were used to turn rain during the day, for blankets at night, and to hold all their food, except coffee. Their food, three times a day for six days a week, consisted solely of bosoli. Their week's ration was the size of a large cannon ball and was carried in a fiber bag wrapped in green banana leaves. At meal time the boys would squat on their haunches, unroll their supply of bosoli, pinch off a bit into a half gourd of water, stir until the thin mixture was milky white and then drink. I tried bosoli but didn't find it palatable. However, the Isthmus Indians evidently find it both sustaining and nourishing. When I learned how meager their fare was, I arranged to have meat and beans parcelled out to all my crew each night for supper.

I delegated one of my Indian mozos to be our hunter. He really did wonders with an old single barrel muzzle-loading shotgun. He frequently bagged a tropical pheasant (which is the size of a small turkey), now and then a peccary and sometimes a rodent which the natives call *perro de agua*, (water dog). Occasionally he brought in the little tropical deer and once he tried to pawn off a monkey on me. I just could not bring myself to eat it, although the Indians seem to relish the meat when well-roasted over the open fire.

My hunter was following me along the trail one day when suddenly I saw several large pheasants in one of the tall trees. I pulled my .45 pistol and started to stalk for a shot. I had no sooner taken a few stealthy steps, than the birds flew out of range. The mozo came up to me and explained that it is impossible to stalk these birds but, on the other hand, it is easy to get within range by shouting, running and thrashing around. Apparently they become confused and instead of flying off, just sit and tremble until a gun is fired. After having had the benefit of my hunter's advice, I was able to kill a number of these large birds with my pistol. They are mighty good eating.

One late afternoon my hunter and I were walking along one of our trails toward camp when the mozo who was ahead motioned for me to stop. I stopped, but saw nothing. Then he raised his shotgun and shot low down into the woods, slightly ahead of us and to our right. As the sound reverber- through the tall trees I glimpsed several wild hogs (javelins) rushing off in different directions. I realized that these large animals — bigger than the Arkansas razorbacks — could not have been seriously wounded by my boy's shot because his gun was loaded with bird shot. So I stood my ground and gaped at a huge boar that had turned back and was running in my general direction along the bank of a small stream. It was not until I could see the boar bristles standing straight up along the ridge of his back and caught the gleam of his long wicked tusks, that I realized my danger. I pulled my pistol and fired at the boar as he charged me head on. Apparently my shot missed — at any rate he kept coming. I shot a second time when he was only a few feet away, but before I could jump out of his way he had bowled me over, his tusks ripping my pants below the knee and gashing my

leg slightly. When I scrambled to my feet there lay the boar only a few feet away, dead. More by accident than good marksmanship, my second shot had passed between his fore shoulders and into his heart. My hunter cut a long stout pole, over which we tied the boar legs with vines, and, trussed up that way, we carried our prize back to camp on our shoulders. I don't know what he weighed but I remember that I staggered along the trail under my end of the pig. The boar's tusks measured over six inches long.

This incident happened on a Saturday afternoon, hence we would not be in the field the next day. Under the circumstances I suggested that my hunter and the other men pack the pig by canoe to our base camp below Filisola where, between my camp supplies and the local villagers, there should be ample facilities to prepare a sure enough barbecue, sufficient for everyone in the vicinity. My boys were all cheerful over the prospects of a real feed and assured me they knew just what to do and how to do it. They suggested that I remain in my up-river camp that night, and they would send a canoe to fetch me back to the base camp by noon the next day. So, it was agreed.

It was mid-morning when the dugout canoe taxi arrived with four sturdy Indian paddlers. Enroute I inquired of the crew what had happened to the pig. I made out, from their signs and poor Spanish, that the pig had been gutted and skinned; then the women had stuffed the belly cavity full of green corn, platanos, mangos, green and red peppers and other fruits and vegetables, and sewed up the carcass in its own hide again. While this butchering was going on, a pit had been dug in the ground several feet deep and a wood fire was set going in the pit. When there was a thick bed of red hot coals, large stones were lowered into the pit. When the stones were steaming hot and the flames of the fire had died away, green banana leaves were thrown over the stones and onto this leafy blanket the pig carcass, also wrapped in banana leaves, was lowered by ropes. When the ropes were withdrawn, the pit was partially filled with fresh earth and the buried carcass was left to slowly simmer and roast overnight.

When I arrived a crowd of about twenty Indian men, women and children gathered around me with smiles and hearty handshakes. They said the feast was ready whenever I was. Accordingly, with some ceremony I gave the word. Boys jumped into the still warm pit and began passing out baskets of dirt to be dumped at one side. Soon the shriveled leaves and singed hide came into view. Then several men took over and with hooks fastened onto poles dragged out the carcass which was laid on fresh banana leaves in the shade of a tree. The burned hide was removed and there was revealed a whole roast pig with steaming juices oozing out of the white meat.

In all my life, I've never had a more succulent barbecue —sweet, juicy, and as tender as a newborn lamb. The stuffing in the belly cavity had given the meat a delicious spicy flavor and aromatic odor. Everyone gorged, everyone was happy, but no one more so than I. It was a real holiday in the tropics, among simple, but friendly, Indian folks.

While on Filisola I observed several different kinds of monkeys but the ones which interested me most were the little fellows with white mutton chop whiskers and the big apelike monkeys that live high in the trees.

Except for their long tails, the "little old men" are but slightly larger than the northern grey squirrel. They travel in groups of a dozen or more — sometimes as many as fifty. I've never seen their nests, if they have any. In daylight they rush around the low brush feeding off fruits, leaves and berries. Whenever I came along the trails the little fellows would chatter and jabber, their whiskers abobbing, as they peeked at me from behind leaves and branches. Now and then, they would gather in a huddle as though in council, only to rush off to another vantage point where they could pelt me with twigs and leaves. To me, they were more fun than the circus, for here they were uncaged and uninhibited, like little people in another world.

The big apelike monkeys were seldom seen other than in a family group. One bright day about noontime, I spied such a family high up in the big trees, at least 75 feet above the ground. Papa was evidently angry at my intrusion on their solitude as he barked and raged and jumped up and down on a limb. Mama appeared concerned lest harm should come to the three little ones which clung to her breast as she sat silently watching papa, now and then glancing down at me. I decided to see what would happen if they were scared. So I fired off my pistol, which made a frightful racket as the sound reverberated through the trees. Immediately, papa monkey started running out along a big branch until it bent way down under his weight, but he hesitated to jump across the great gap to the branches of the next big tree. He began jumping and scolding, harder and harder as the branch sprang up and down in a great arc. Finally he leaped the gap and clung to the branches of the far tree. Then mama monkey, with her babies, advanced out on the limb where papa had been. There she stopped and called to him—back and forth they seemingly argued. I surmised that she felt she could not make this great leap with the babies hanging to her breast. They must have concocted a plan; at any rate, mama began jumping on her limb and papa on his. The branches were now describing big arcs, the higher one on which mama hung almost meeting the lower one on which papa clung. It resembled the flying trapeze act in the circus. Suddenly, papa swung out on his upswing and caught hold of mama on her down-swing. They clung together as they held to their respective branches. Then, believe it or not, the babies scrambled over onto papa, who let go of mama and swung back into his tree. Mama then executed a solo swing out and over to the other tree as papa had done at first. The monkey family, reunited by passing their babies over a living bridge, chattered off out of sight through the tree tops. Having witnessed this unusual episode, I shall always feel that these ape-like monkeys on Filisola not only think but must have a comprehensive language of their own.

One Sunday I borrowed a dugout canoe and paddled across the Rio Uspanapa to visit a large lake on the far side, only a short way inland. I was alone, for I was merely adventuring and not working. With my machete I cut a trail through the brush from the river to lakeside. Flocks of wild water fowl got up from the reeds and shallows as I appeared. Also, to my consternation, many huge crocodiles slithered over the sandy beach and into the water. I had been told that many natives had lost their lives along the streams and in the swamps of the Isthmus country by being dragged into the water by crocodiles. Some of the "crocs" I saw that Sunday must have been at least twenty feet long from snout to tip of tail. The sight of so many of these huge, ugly monsters caused me to reconsider whether my desire for adventure was really worth the risk. While pondering, I decided to rest on a convenient log lying half buried in the sand well up from the water's edge. I backed up to my log and sat down hard. The log moved. I jumped up and away as grandpa croc angrily made for the water. No more sitting down for me in that spot — henceforth I would do my pondering on my two feet well out in the clear.

As I walked along I noticed a mound of sand some yards from the water's edge and from this mound there were two well-marked trails leading to and from the water. Here, then, must be a nest of crocodile eggs and the trail must be that made by the mother's tail as she dragged herself onto the beach to deposit her eggs and then returned to the water. I dug into the mound and sure enough there was about a bushel of crocodile eggs, probably not more than a day old. Once the mother croc has emptied her egg sack she covers the nest with sand and abandons it, leaving the sun to hatch the brood and the brood to fend for themselves. It's quite a sight to see hundreds of freshly hatched crocs, only a few inches long, snapping their tiny jaws and shaking their little tails as they scamper to the shallow waters in search of food and cover. At that stage the croc is a prey for land animals, large fish and water birds and the mortality rate among infant crocs is high.

Once I was tempted to try eating some fresh laid crocodile eggs. They are about the size of a large hen's egg but have a leathery skin on the outside instead of the hard limey shell of birds. Whether fried, scrambled or boiled croc's eggs all taste the same to me—terribly oily and fishy. While I don't recommend them to the American gourmet, they are certainly highly prized as food and much sought after by primitive peoples of many lands.

One of my camps on Filisola was set back from a small stream of water inland some distance from the Rio Uspanapa. There my native boys had built me a bamboo and palm house. Juan and his family lived nearby, but there were no other humans for many miles. I had picked this location because of the high ground along a pleasant little stream and also because there was a pool in the stream which should make a good swimming hole. It was a nice set-up in every way. When I came in at night tired, hot and dirty, I'd strip and take a plunge into the pool first thing and then dry off, take a shot of quinine with a glass of wine before sitting down to a hot Mexican supper prepared by Juan's wife.

One evening when I took my plunge Juan's two small boys came down to the bank and sat there silently. I asked them to come on in. I liked kids and was lonesome, but they shook their heads and ran off. This performance was repeated night after night for a week or more before I asked their father if there was any particular reason why the boys would not swim with me. "Well," said Juan, "my boys like you very much indeed, in fact they think you are a very brave man, but jefe they are scared to go in that pool."

"Why are they scared?," I asked.

"Because," said Juan, "the biggest crocodile in these parts lives in that pool."

After that explanation I did my bathing in a bucket as long as I remained in that camp.

These vignettes of jungle life would not be complete without the story of my finding the fresh foot print of the "prehistoric" horse.

As mentioned elsewhere, shortly after graduating from college I was assigned by my company to explore the oil prospects of Filisola. I was so fresh from the study of paleontology that the finding of any fossils or other signs of prehistoric life was exciting, for it is by means of such evidence that the geologist determines the age of the sedimentary formations which make up so much of the earth's crust.

Students of vertebrate paleontology learn that the horse, as we know it today, evolved from a small four-footed ancestor of antelope size, having five toes on each foot. Fossil remains of these little five-toed horses have been found in the United States, but, I believe, nowhere else in the world. Each of these five toes resembled the large hoofs of the modern horse. Furthermore, the modern horse, besides having a large hoof, actually still has the remnants of four other toes concealed in the lower leg structure.

Sometime before the dawn of man in the Americas the horse migrated from this continent to other parts of the world. Horses have been known in Asia and parts of Europe since the earliest days of recorded history. However, there is no record which would indicate that any of the Indians in the Western Hemisphere had ever heard of or seen a horse before the days of Columbus and Cortez. How did these ancient horses migrate from the Americas and why did they all migrate — if they all did? For the most part, man is still able only to speculate as to the how and the why.

When I arrived in the Isthmus jungle, I could not help but contemplate that somewhere in the remote parts of the Americas there might yet be found a living throwback of the five-toed horse. Maybe, I might be so lucky as to find a living prehistoric horse in Mexico.

It was under such circumstances that I began my exploration in the jungles of Filisola.

My survey was nearly complete, except for considerable swamp area in the southern part of the hacienda. Progress was slow because of the morass of bush, cane and water, through which we had to proceed with caution, having due regard for crocodiles and snakes. Because of the terrain and long distance from camp, I was working alone, except for my Indian helper and guide. One day about noon, he came upon fresh footprints in a mud flat, deep in the swamp. He called the spoor to my attention. It was then that I got the thrill of a young geologist's life. It must be the footprint of a pre-historic horse for these were the unmistakable prints of a foot having four tiny hoof-like toes and the faint imprint of a fifth hoof, evidently atrophied. I asked my man if he had ever seen the animal that made such a track.

"Si, Senor!"

"What does it look like?"

"Well," said Juan, "it's bigger than a burro but smaller than a mule."

"Does it have horns?" I asked.

"No, Senor!"

"Does it have a tail like a horse or cow?" I queried.

"Si, Senor!"

"What color is it?" I asked.

Juan replied, "It is a kind of grey-brown color and the hair is short."

By that time I really was excited. I asked Juan by what name this animal was known locally. He said *Anti Burro* (which literally means, "Before the burro"). Then I was certain I had actually found a living specimen of the prehistoric horse. I feverously sketched the footprint in my notebook, carefully measuring all the dimensions, and recorded the geographic location of the find and the description of the animal as given to me by Juan. I would send this record on to my college professors for identification as soon as I got back to the company's main office in Tampico.

But I never did mail out that record — I still have it in my archives.

Still elated over my significant find of a fresh footprint of a "prehistoric" horse, I could not keep the important news to myself—I had to tell someone. So, when I arrived in Minititlan I began to discreetly query others who had been in the jungle country for sometime, as to whether or not they had ever seen or heard of the Anti Burro. To my chagrin these old-timers said, "Yes, it is fairly common in the jungle swamps."

"Well, what is it—does it have any other name?" I asked.

"Son," they said, "what is an Anti Burro to the Indians hereabouts may be better known to you as a tapir." Still incredulous, I pressed them to describe the footprint of the tapir. My ego was entirely deflated when the old-timers' description of the tapir track coincided exactly with the sketch I had made of Anti Burro's spoor in the wet mud.

My rare footprint of a living prehistoric horse was only the track of the common tapir.

8

Siege of Tampico

Now, looking back over 50 years, the headlined "Siege of Tampico," seems more like a comic opera episode than serious warfare. However, at the time, Tampiquenos and foreigners alike were tense with apprehension lest there be an all-out battle in and around Mexico's largest seaport city. A real siege could cause great suffering and many casualties to non-combatants. Such an eventuality was envisaged by other nations, as British, American, Dutch and German gunboats gathered off Tuxpam and in the Panuco River off Tampico.

Victoriano Huerta had become President of Mexico in February, 1913, following the assassination of President Francisco Madero and Vice President Jose Maria Pino Suarez. In the early fall of that year, four of the greatest guerrilla leaders, with their armies and retinues, took the field against the Federals under Huerta. These four were Venustiano Carranza of Coahuila, who controlled northeast Mexico; Pancho Villa in Chihuahua and Durango (northwest Mexico); Emiliano Zapata, called "The Attila of the South," in Morelos and Guerrero; and Alvaro Obregon of Sonora, who controlled the fiercest fighters in Mexico, the Yaqui Indians. There was no agreement binding the revolutionaries, but they were all loosely united against their common enemy—Huerta. Their battle cry was, "Death to Huerta, down with the foreigners, Mexico for the Mexicans."

The Zapatistas were a peasant army. Even on a raid they dressed in their peon garb, having only laid down the hoe and taken up the rifle. One day they would attack a hacienda and the next day they would be back in their houses and fields.

The Obregonistas, the Carransistas and the Villistas had a more military look on the march. They had uniforms of sorts—all sorts—and were well-armed except for artillery.

Anita Breuner in her book, *The Wind that Swept Mexico*, published in 1943, includes a word picture of these revolutionary armies—so vivid and so characteristic of the times:

The main battles were along the railroads, with advance attacks often carried out in combination with railroad men who had waived their payroll and pension rights and had come in as revolutionaries. A locomotive might be speeded ahead, heavily armed, moving fast into town like a tank; or an old engine or a handcar might be turned into a torpedo by loading it with explosives and sending it crashing into a Federal train.

When these armies moved it was like a mass migration. They carried families, three layers deep: some inside the box cars, some on top and others, mostly the boys and young men, in hammocks slung between the wheels. Tortillas were ground and baked on fires in oil cans along the whole top of the trains, and dogs and babies accommodated themselves in the warmest corners inside. The age span for soldiering was from about seven to seventy. Boys under ten were usually buglers, drummers or couriers, and did sentry duty, too. Beyond twelve no one questioned their place as full fledged soldiers. The women, though their job was foraging, cooking and looking after the wounded, pitched in and fought if they felt like it. If a woman's husband was killed she could attach herself to some other man or take over his uniform and gun herself. Almost every troop had a famous lady colonel or lady captain, a husky earringed girl armed to the teeth, and among headlong reckless fighters one of the first. All these people, Zapatistas, followers of Obregon or Carranza, painters and buglers, Yaqui Indians and mule drivers, were known as Constitutionalists—opposed to the Federals whose reluctant bayonets upheld Huerta. Within a year, despite all international calculations to the contrary, they had wiped the Federals out in three-fourths of Mexico.

Such were the conditions in Mexico in November 1913 when General Carranza initiated his Veracruz campaign by mobilizing a small force under Candido Aguilar to move against Tuxpam and from there northward to occupy the South Country oil fields. Thirty days later the Carransistas moved in on Tampico from the north and south. The "Siege of Tampico" had received much advance publicity, both in Mexico and abroad. War correspondents and warships from many countries flocked to vantage points in the vicinity.

Neither the attack on Tuxpam, the occupation of the oil fields nor the "Siege of Tampico" were military maneuvers of any great historic moment. Certainly the actualities of the fighting were not as momentous as the current press portrayed. Considering the large amount of powder and shot expended, the casualties on both sides were very small. However, some of the corollary events and happenings were of sufficient interest to have been mentioned in letters written at the time from Tampico to "my dear parents." Portions of those letters are quoted below.

These letters were written primarily to allay the fears and worry of my parents. Actually there was very considerable danger to civilian life and property all during the siege.

Tampico, Tamps.
Nov. 23, 1913

I wonder if you all have been getting the latest war news in the State papers, if not, probably you are much more at ease mentally than otherwise. It seems that even the Mexican newspapers are ignoring the recent invasion of the Rebel forces into the Oil Fields of Veracruz. Their ignorance is due, no doubt, to the fact that if the real condition of affairs became public property, invasion would result. To be brief, the last ten days' situation has been as follows:

The 'Carransistas' under Gen. Candido Aguilar moved upon the Port of Tuxpam where they engaged the Federal troops. However, owing to the Rebel's lack of any artillery, they were repulsed, even after gaining parts of the town and fell back onto our oil camps, making Tanhuijo their headquarters. During the Tuxpam fight, it was reported that the Mexicans had fired on a tugboat flying the British flag and carrying an English Vice-Consul on board—this news was wired to the U. S. Battleship Louisiana, which, on hearing same, immediately embarked 70 Marines with machine guns on lighters, and started to land troops, but, before the boys could land the real truth was flashed to the ship and the sailors were accordingly wig-wagged to return. If the Marines had landed, old Uncle Sam would have had to invade at once. Aguilar, after establishing his 500 or 600 men in Tanhuijo, sallied forth and proceeded to take Tamiahua and every oil camp in the vicinity, Los Naranjos included. This done, he took over our telephone line, and then tied up every launch the company had. When the Rebels had all the gringos and the oil properties at their mercy they very politely requested horses, arms, etc. and $100,000.00 each from the Aguila and Huasteca Petroleum Companies—all of which was given them. So that is the way the affair now stands—the Rebels are still in all of the oil camps, literally living off the oil companies.

All the time these events were going on, I was in the field trying to work—every day I met Rebels and exchanged courtesies with them, while, at night, I slept well after having my man hide my horses and saddles in the monte. However, one day they did take my little pacing horse, but I bought him back for ten pesos. As I said above I was trying to work yet, in fact, I did not do much. I became acquainted with General (Doctor) R. Cardenas and easy like, requested a written pass from him in order that I might not be molested—he refused —and the next day I was stopped in my survey. So, soon pulled up stakes and beat it to Tampico.

Of one thing we are sure, so long as the States do not intervene there is little or no danger to foreign life—but should Wilson finally decide upon such an action, me for a gunboat. Tomorrow I expect to go back down into the country with Mr. Dewey (General Supt. of the camps) in his fast boat the "Peggy." We intend to ride thru the camps and make a decision as to whether or not it is safe to go on with field operations at present.

Tampico, Tamps.
Dec. 16, 1913

I expect by this time you all are pretty well worried over the recent happenings in Mexico, since the actual rebellion has now centered around Tampico and more especially the events of the last few days.

No doubt the papers have been saying—"Tampico taken by Carranza," "Hundreds of Americans forced to flee for their lives to the battleships," "The streets of the oil city run with blood," "Many foreigners killed," etc., which is every whit bull. In order that you all may really know the truth I will recite briefly the doings of the past weeks.

Early Wednesday morning (Dec. 9th) at 2 A.M. to be exact, Mr. F. C. Phillips came through the corridors of the office building (where I now have a room on the fourth floor) shouting for all Englishmen to proceed at once to the British merchantman lying off the Custom House as the Rebels were about to enter the city. All of the monocled ones left the city and boarded their ship, making such a noise in their departure that the few Americans left in the building could not sleep. In the morning there was considerable excitement on the streets for it was learned that a Rebel force of 6,000 men were within four miles of the city—but as yet there had been no shots exchanged by either the Federals or Carransistas.

About 11 o'clock (Dec. 10th) the first skirmish began and a rapid fire was continued all day long. From the top of our building through my telescope I could plainly see the trenches of the National troops and could hear the sharp putt of the Mauser rifles. Later in the afternoon the cannon began to speak only to be followed by the rapid putt-putt-putt of machine guns. Altogether it was a grand sight and sound. Every once in a while the "Bravo" (Mexican cruiser) would send a shot whistling over the city into the hills to the west, where the Rebels were located.

Immediately after the fighting began, arrangements were made for foreigners to go on board the ships in the harbor and others to lodge in the Aguila company's building, for fear of rioting in case the Rebels came in. I acted on the house committee and as a guard at night. After nightfall, the big doors of the offices were sandbagged and armed guards and lookouts were placed at all entrances and on the roof and so passed the first night of the siege. Over 90 women and 150 men were trying to sleep in our building amid the crackle and roar of a real battle just outside the city. The next day was a repetition of fighting, first the Federals and then the Rebels gained advantage and in the meantime two American cruisers, the "Chester" and "Tacoma," and one German and one English cruiser sailed up the river opposite the town.

In order to better cope with any lengthy siege, our building was put under martial law with a Captain in absolute charge, a Lieutenant and three sergeants. Of the latter, I was first Sergeant in charge of four guards (our hours were 12 to 2 A.M. and P.M. and 6 to 8 A.M. and P.M.). As a body, this military organization could dictate to everyone except Dr. Hayes. By so doing, the building was patrolled both night and day with a body of 20 men always at command in case of emergency. This move was entirely precautionary.

As I said before, the fight of the 11th was much like the 10th as far as we could see from the city. Likewise the day of the 12th was merely a repetition but with advantage to the Federals. Early on Saturday, the Rebels retreated and ceased firing so that there was a quiet over the entire vicinity.

Immediately the rumors that the forces of Carranza had fallen back were officially known and confirmed, people began to sally forth to the battlefield. Hundreds of Federal dead were burned on the spot making quite an impressive sight and one not often seen. The region of fighting was scattered with exploded shells and fragments of wearing apparel—so that the curiosity seeking American could pick up relics to his heart's content. So that is the way things stand today. The Federals are boozing in celebration while the Rebels have retired to Altamira some 14 miles distant. No one knows whether the Rebels will attack again or not, but the general consensus is that the Federal forces garrisoned here now can withstand any attack they may make.

The "Morro Castle," a Ward Liner, has just sailed into the harbor to take off the refugees to the States. Personally, I should like to go even if only for a vacation over Christmas. The way things stand at present, it will be impossible for me to go to the field for a time, so I expect to stick around town at least over the holidays.

You might be interested to note that I have two passes for myself, horse and side arms given to me personally by General C. Aguilar and First Capt. Guerro—in addition I know Col. Mariel, also a Carranssista, besides have been in conference with Gen. C. Aguilar's Staff—so that there is little or no fear for my safety in the Rebel ranks, while the Federals dare not harm any foreigners for policy's sake.

So dear people do not worry about me as I will not stay here unless I am needed when the real danger comes, so please rest as easy as you can and try to believe about one-half of the news the papers print—the U. S. Gunboats are always in port in case of trouble.

Tampico, Tamps.
March 28th, 1914

By the time you get this no doubt the "second attack" on Tampico will be a matter of history. Yesterday, however, as we put-put-putted up the lagoon from La Pena we could hear the boom of the cannon and the crackle of side arms. The engagement took place about three miles from Tampico, near a place called, "Dona Cecilia." Today, the Federals claimed they caused the Rebels to retreat and indeed it looks that way for no firing has gone on all day. Here in town there is not the least evidence of fear, people throng the streets and all stores are open—no doubt a good deal of this brave spirit may be accredited to the fact that gunboats of all the "first" nations of the world fairly swarm the harbor. Personally, I do not believe there is any danger and so am continuing my ordinary duties as usual. What the eventual outcome will be is pretty hard to say.

During the "Siege of Tampico," several of my American associates were minor casualties—nothing serious, but amusing.

During the fighting, when the Federals were lofting rifle fire over the city inland toward the Rebels, two of my friends were walking down one of the narrow streets, keeping close to the buildings to avoid being hit by stray bullets. Suddenly, one fellow clasped his backsides then squared off and struck his companion a lusty blow with his fist saying angrily, "Why did you kick me?" "I did no such thing," said the other. Whereupon they stopped in their tracks to investigate. To their amazement they found the injured man had been hit by a spent bullet which lodged in the heavy leather wallet in his back pocket. There was no blood—only a bruised behind.

Another time one of my colleagues was viewing the battleground through field glasses from the top of one of Tampico's tallest buildings. He was comfortably standing behid a cement parapet gazing out over the lagoon in back of the city and facing the Rebel forces entrenched in Dona Cecilia, several miles distant. Suddenly, his Texas hat went flying off his head. When he picked it up he found a bullet hole clean through the crown, only inches above his forehead.

One amusing incident took place between the opposing forces. The Federals were dug-in northwest of the city in what was known as the Aguila Colony. The rebels were on a hill close in to the Colony property along the same main road. A tram line lay along this road from Tampico

to beyond the Rebel lines. Evidently the Federals planned
to blast the Rebel front line to kingdom come by sending
an explosive packed tram car hurtling down the track.
But the plan went awry because of gravity. The rail torpedo was got off all right, fuse sputtering, down the hill
as fast as man power could push it. Away the torpedo
speeded, faster and faster, the Federals yelling and waving.
Like a rocket it hurtled down the track to the bottom of
the slope between the battle lines. On up the opposite
slope the car of explosives sped, but slower and slower as
it went upgrade. Now the Rebels were yelling and waving,
too. Neither side was shooting. All was excitement as both
sides watched the progress of the torpedo. Just short of the
hilltop occupied by the Rebels, the car came to a halt and
then slowly gathered momentum as it slid back down toward
the Federal position—the fuse sputtering all the while. Just
as the torpedo reached the bottom of the slope, halfway between the lines, the explosion occurred. There were no casualties, except for a skinny old horse which had been grazing
along the roadside.

9

Cow Dung

In the early 1900's the oil industry began to turn to
geology as a tool in the search for petroleum reservoirs.
Strangely enough geologists and petroleum engineers were
generally accepted in foreign exploration before they were
commonly employed in the United States. A considerable
emphasis toward the use of geology in the field of "finding"
oil abroad was due to Dr. C. W. Hayes, formerly head of the
United States Geological Survey, who became the head of
Lord Cowdrey's oil empire in Mexico. Dr. Hayes set the
pattern of using geologists in large numbers to survey the oil
prospects over all the British company's vast holdings in
Veracruz and the Isthmus of Tehuantepec.

However, drillers and operators from the States were slow
to accept geology as a useful tool. They had much more faith
in the "wiggle stick" and "oil sense" than in the observations
of "mud slingers" and "ridge runners," as they commonly
called young field geologists. These oldtimers in Mexico had
their instructions to cooperate with the geologists both on and
off the derrick floor, but for many years their cooperation was

125

more in the nature of toleration. They kidded and baited the geologists—short of running into difficulties with management—whenever and wherever possible.

Such was the oil geologist's status in Mexico when I joined Dr. Hayes' company in 1912, fresh out of college. A few months later, I was assigned to a field job in the vicinity of the company's great oil camp at Potrero del Llano. It was there I met Sam Weaver, drilling superintendent for all Lord Cowdrey's oil activities in northern Veracruz—a big man filling a big job.

Sam had been a truck driver in West Virginia. One day he delivered a load of oil field pipe to a drilling contractor by the name of John Slater, who remarked, "Son, you're too husky and strong to be a truck driver all your life. Why don't you get a job that pays big and has a future?"

Sam said, "Dad, you tell me how and where and I'll do it."

"All right," replied Slater. "Report to me tomorrow morning early, and I'll sign you on as helper on one of my drilling rigs. Some day you'll get to be a driller and then you can go places."

Sam reported to Slater the next morning and made good. Now, some years later, he was holding the top drilling job for one of the largest oil companies in Mexico. He knew all the techniques then known of drilling with either rotary or cable tools. Also, he knew how to handle his crews, whether drillers or roughnecks, regardless of nationality. He was blunt of speech in the field but in mixed company his conversation sparkled with wit and good humor. Sam's Spanish was the peon variety — words, phrases and idioms learned by ear after he came to Mexico — not always polite and seldom grammatical, but readily understood by the Mexican laborers and artisans in the oil fields. The more liquor Sam had under his belt the more fluent his Spanish.

I liked Sam Weaver and he encouraged me to visit him, either in his office or at his home, whenever I was in camp. We used to talk by the hour about his experiences in the oil business in the States and especially in Mexico. I knew he had been in charge of the drilling of many "gusher" wells so I prodded him for details of the drilling game. Reciprocally, Sam wanted to learn about how a geologist determined the whereabouts of underground structures favorable to the accumulation of hydrocarbons, and plied me with all kinds of questions about my work. However, in the presence of his crews, Sam usually joked about geology and geologists.

Some months after I left Potrero on another assignment, Sam Weaver resigned from the British company to become general field superintendent of an American company which was prospecting for oil in the Haciendo Alamo on the Tuxpam River about 12 miles south of Potrero. His new employers had drilled several failures on what appeared to be a most likely prospect. There were many surface oil seeps around Alamo but all the holes drilled so far had encountered the "pay" limestone at relatively shallow depths and found large volumes of hot salt water but little or no oil. The American company had geologists in the field and I believe, though I don't know for certain, that all the "failures" had been located by them. No matter who located those dry holes, it seems certain that Sam had stipulated in his agreement with the American company, when employed, that he would locate the next well to be drilled.

Shortly after Sam arrived in Alamo several of his company's directors visited camp. They knew of Sam's excellent record with the British company and they also were mindful of the stipulation in his contract with their company. Under the circumstances, since the tools on the last dry hole were being rigged down, these directors pressed Sam as to the location for "his well." At the time, they were all sitting on the porch of the camp guest bunkhouse, facing a broad expanse of pasture in which cattle were wandering about cropping the tall lush grass or lying in the shade of the occasional tree contentedly chewing their cuds. It was the quiet hour of approaching dusk after a very hot and sultry day.

Sam didn't immediately reply to inquiries about the location for the next test. He sat for five or ten minutes without speaking as he gazed out on the pastoral scene. Finally, he got to his feet, picked up a narrow, straight stick and a short-handled axe and strode off toward the pasture. His porch audience saw him climb over the pasture fence and then stride toward some of the young cattle. He singled out and followed one of the yearlings around and around. At last, the yearling stopped a moment and then dashed off with tail up as Sam came close. Sam stopped where the yearling had stopped and his axe flashed up and down as though he were driving a stake into the ground.

Naturally, his audience was curious about what Sam had done and he was met with a volley of questions. Sam grinned and appeared completely satisfied with himself and what he had done. At last one of the directors said, "Sam, come now, tell us what you were up to out there in the pasture chasing cattle around."

"Well, Boss," replied Sam, "it's this away—you-all been prodding me to locate the next hole—well, I've gone and done it and it will be a discovery gusher." The group laughed and wanted to know his reason for driving the location stake where he did. "Well, I'll tell you," said Sam, "all your geologists' locations have so far resulted in dry holes and I've listened to the BS of geologists so many years that I thought we'd try heifer dung for a change, just for luck."

Believe it or not, that American company did drill their next test hole on the precise pasture site staked by Sam, and it eventually was completed as a gusher well, the first and largest producer in the Alamo field.

That is the story of the Alamo discovery well as it was told to me many years ago.

IO

Hunting Deer with
Pen Knife and Handkerchief

It happened down in Mexico during the revolutionary days, about 1920. I was general agent for the Mexican Gulf Oil Company at the time. Consequently, it was my responsiblity to see that visiting officals from the home office were properly entertained. On this occasion my guests were the company's purchasing agent and a top man from an oil well supply company. After a quick tour of the oil terminals along the Panuco River and a running trip to the oil camps in the Panuco-Topila area and in the South Country, our VIPs were of a mind to do some fresh water fishing along the upper reaches of the Tamesi River. There had been rumors of trout having been caught upcountry near the old custom house (now abandoned), on the border between the states of Tamaulipas and Veracruz. The area, near the ford of the Tamesi River, was reported to be desolated of settlers because of once frequent revolutionary marauding. However, since no recent raids had been reported we felt it would be safe to try out luck.

Equipped with tackle and provisions for several days, our party headed north by auto from Tampico for the hacienda Chocoy. There we picked up a Mexican guide and the American manager of the hacienda with his Ford. We headed southwest across the plains, following almost extinct cart and horse trails which skirted around the low hills. Some of these brush and tree-covered knolls "smelled" of deer and wild turkey. I had brought along a repeating shotgun just in case, but we all were too anxious to try for game fish in the fast waters of the Tamesi to tarry en route for other sport. It was a long, dusty, tiresome trip and nearly dusk when we arrived at our destination.

Two large customs warehouses and several smaller buildings still stood at the ford, all of which appeared to have been abandoned for some years. As we pulled up we could see no sign of life at first — only the stark bullet-spattered adobe walls of the buildings. All the smaller structures had been burned out, either by gunfire or incendiary, but the warehouses appeared not to have been fired, although rust and storm had collapsed great sections of the corrugated iron roofs. Altogether it was a scene of desolation, somewhat eerie and foreboding.

Finally, we spied a thin spiral of smoke arising from behind the brush, indicating to us that possibly someone was living nearby. In answer to our shouts, a middle-aged swarthy Mexican, complete with machete dangling from his sash, hesitatingly emerged and declared he was the official caretaker of this government property. He was much relieved to see that we were obviously not soldiers and carried no rifles. With a smile, he said, "Buenos tardes amigos—vaya con Dios." We replied in kind and asked if he could furnish our party with food and lodging for the night. Throwing up his hands and rolling his eyes toward the sky, the caretaker protested that before God he could not give us either food or bed—"Nosotros no tenemos nada." Well, his nondescript appearance and the looks of the empty buildings certainly vouched for his veracity. So, without argument, for the night was falling rapidly, we asked him if we could makeshift our own grub and bed down in one of the old warehouses. The caretaker agreed and immediately said his *mujer* could bring us hot coffee and he would bring us candles and empty beer bottles for candle sticks.

With that we unloaded our duffle and then inspected the buildings to determine which might best serve as our "hotel." We chose one of the warehouses which appeared to have more roof in place than the others. It was a huge structure, approximately 40 feet wide by 160 feet long, with thick mud walls rising up about 15 feet from the ground. The inside was divided into four equal-size sections by mud partitions extending up to the eave line. Large framed doorways connected the sections but the heavy wood double doors had been removed. The exterior doors were in place and locked and the window openings were barred and shuttered. Apparently, we would be secure from molestation or attack by man or animal from the outside, although vulnerable to the weather, insect life, bats and rats on the inside. Until the caretaker had opened the exterior doors and windows, our chosen abode looked dark and dismal. We could hear the rats scurrying overhead under the eaves and along the roof beams. Many small lizards darted over the hard-packed dirt floor and up along the walls.

As quickly as possible, we marshalled in our belongings and got at the job of setting up furniture. We found scores of empty kerosene boxes and, standing in one corner, the unhinged interior doors. One large door laid flat on top of four upright boxes made a splendid table. Other doors were similarly placed on boxes for use as cots. Springless and hard though these beds would be, we all agreed they were better than sleeping on the dirt floor admidst accumulated filth of years and its insect inhabitants. Other upended boxes were arranged around the room to serve as chairs and night stands. We were proud of our handiwork and, when candles were lit, the gloomy barnlike place became quite cheerful.

The mujer soon came along with a large pot of coffee, some enameled ware plates, a few knives, forks and spoons and, to our great delight, a large stack of hot tortillas. When our tins of meat, fruit and jam had been opened, we fell to. All of us were hungry and we silently shoveled in and chomped. Insects, attracted by the candlelight, flew in the open windows in clouds. The mosquitoes were a noisy nuisance, but the silent moths were worse—they got all over the opened food on the table, even rode the food into our mouths, and fluttered all around our faces. Finally, with our hunger assuaged, all candles were blown out and pipes and cigarettes were lit. Soon most of our pesky insect visitors departed and at last we were at peace with the world.

It was only natural that we old-timers should begin to tell stories of the revolutionary days in Mexico for the benefit of our unsophisticated American guests. Here, in these battle scarred, smoke-begrimed walls, lighted only by burning cigarettes or the flare of a match, these yarns came alive. The related harrowing incidents of yesteryear in remote places seemed to the listeners to have occurred only yesterday in this very area. In that atmosphere of mystery and suspense it was agreed we all should try for some sleep.

Almost fully clothed, we stretched out on our respective beds and hoped for the best. For a while there was a deal of grunting and turning as each fellow tried to find the most comfortable position on those hard, unupholstered door-beds. However, it was not long until the only sound was that of snores, the scurrying of rats and occasionally the swish of bats on their nightly prowl for the lingering insect.

Old-timer oil men in Mexico learned to sleep fitfully. Their subconscious mind became attuned to alarms—they could "feel" danger. Since, during my years in the country, I had been exposed to actual and rumored ambush on the road and night raids on camps, I was one to sleep lightly. I could not help feeling that something was going to happen. Soon it did. Two or more rats evidently got to fighting for the right of way over one of the cross beams, and one big rat fell off "kuplunk" on top of the generous belly of a VIP. The injured party let out a loud yell that we were being attacked. Everyone roused and rolled off onto the floor prepared to run to the monte. A hurried investigation disclosed what the real trouble was and so we returned to bed, rather sheepishly. The night wore on and again the night life began to prowl and play. There was another rat combat on an overhead joist. This time the unfortunate rat fell and landed inside the upturned cap of the other visitor. Round and round, inside the cap ran the rat, jingling and jangling the mess of keys, coins and whatnot that had been placed there by the owner. It was startling to all and frightening to some. Again, we were aroused and cussing. This incident was too much for our visitors who said they'd rather be eaten up by the mosquitoes outside in the car than to be scared to death inside on boards. So, outside the two of them went. They crawled into the seats of the old Buick and settled down in the chill air to spend the rest of the night with their raincoats pulled over their heads.

There were no further outbreaks of consequence but we were all glad when the dawn broke. When those of us who

had remained inside went out to rouse our friends in the autos, we found them so chilled and cramped that it took them a good half hour to straighten up and get going.

After hot coffee, our party descended on the white waters and quiet pools of the Tamesi. For hours, we whipped the stream repeatedly with all sorts of flies, plugs and spinners without a single strike. Disgusted, we returned to our warehouse camp and decided, after a council of war, to return at least to Chocoy and maybe to Tampico.

Early that morning I had seen fresh deer tracks in a little cornfield near the caretaker's house. So, when we were loaded and about to leave, I proposed that we stop at one of those likely deer haunts in the hopes that we might at least return with venison or turkey. It was agreed. Consequently, we stopped our two-car caravan several hundred yards short of one of those tree and brush covered knolls. I got out with my loaded gun and walked softly forward. Sure enough, upon reaching the knoll I could see a faint narrow animal trail stretching away into the cover. I'd gone about a hundred feet or so along the winding trail before I noticed a movement in the brush ahead. After further advance of a few steps I saw the white tail of a deer. Realizing that I had no hope of getting where I could make a front or side shot at the deer, I fired a load of buckshot at its rear. Immediately the animal bounded out of sight. Certain that I had made a hit I ran, gun in hand, in the direction the deer had gone. As I came out into a little clearing I saw the deer lying on a brush heap, blood spurting out of his drooping head. He struggled to get to his feet as he heard me approach but was too weak and fell over on his side quietly. Well, I thought, now that I've bagged the buck, why not go for the doe which should be hereabouts. However, as I started to move further into the brush, it occurred to me that maybe the deer was only stunned and might not be dying. I took out my handkerchief and tightly bound together the deer's rear feet—without any protest from the animal. Confident now that my game could not run even though it should revive, I set off once more for the doe.

Somehow, it didn't dawn on me that any other deer in the vicinity would have been startled by the noise of the shot and subsequent confusion and would, no doubt, now be far away. I trudged along the trail for ten or fifteen minutes before giving up and returning to the clearing. Imagine my surprise and chagrin to note, when the brush heap came into view, that my dying deer was now struggling to gain its feet, head up and eyes bright. Of course, the intrepid hunter would have raised his gun and fired a *coup de grace* at once, but not me. I dropped my gun on the ground, ran to the brush heap and jumped astride the deer. It struggled like a bucking bronco but I held on, my left arm locked around its neck in a sort of half nelson. Now what to do—there was my gun some twenty feet away, the handkerchief had become untied from around the deer's legs, and I had neither my hunting knife nor pistol. As the deer struggled, I could see that my shot had only stunned the animal—one or maybe two bullets had creased its head but apparently none had reached a vital organ. I had to do something and quickly, or my party would have no venison today. Suddenly, I thought of my pen knife. If I could get that out of my pocket and open it, possibly I could sever the deer's jugular. With my free right hand, I found the pen knife and brought it up to my teeth, with which I opened the inch and a half long blade. Then, holding the deer's head up and back as far as I could, I stuck the knife into the animal's throat where I thought the vein ought to be. Nothing happened—there was no large outpouring of blood. I tried again and still no result. Then I started sawing on the windpipe but still no big vein. With all this the deer was obviously getting more and more unhappy and consequently struggling the harder. The weaker I got, the stronger the deer got. Finally, as I relaxed my

butchering attempt the deer made a grand leap and threw me off. In a wink the animal was up and gone, breath whistling from his partly severed windpipe. I scrambled to my feet, still clutching the pen knife, grabbed my gun and took out after the deer. For some distance into the brush I could follow his trail by drops of blood and broken branches. I desperately wanted that deer for I knew he must eventually die from my knife wounds, if not from the bullets. But the trail became fainter and fainter until, after nearly an hour's search, I realized the chase was hopeless.

I found my way out to the cars and told my fishing friends what had happened. They were so skeptical that I led them back to the brush pile and showed them my hankerchief which lay there, the blood stains on the scrambled brush and my bloody pen knife. I even pantomimed the whole episode, but my friends grinned their disbelief. However, they did help me look again in the nearby tangle of undergrowth just in case the deer had fallen under cover. All to no avail, so we walked back to the cars and were soon on the road. We stopped overnight in the hacienda house at Chocoy where the manager was most generous with food and drink, a hot bath all around and real beds to sleep on.

The next day we completed our journey to Tampico. Evidently my American VIP friends were much amused over the incident. At any rate, word of my hunting exploit soon got all around the industry circles—it was even told in the press. "Hamilton, the mighty deer hunter—disdains gun—uses only pen knife and handkerchief," were the headlines.

In subsequent years I have had occasion to tell this story several times among congenial groups and always I have sensed a feeling of disbelief amongst my listeners. People are funny that way.

I I

Fish and Pests

The Rio Panuco was discovered by the captains of
Cortez some 450 years ago. The Spanish adventurers
sailed up this mighty stream for many miles and then carried
on their exploration by dugout canoe as far west as the Tamasopa Mountains. They navigated the tributary streams, now
known as the Tamesi and the Moctezuma, along the eastern
Cordilleras. The early conquistadores likened the Panuco River
system, in size and importance, to that of the Rio Grande.
However, the mouth of the Panuco was so shallow that vessels
drawing more than a few feet could not safely cross the shift-
ing sand bars. Native Indian tribes had established a village
on some high ground in the marshes along the north bank of
the Panuco, upstream several miles from its mouth, which
they called Tampico. This village did not become important
as a trading post until the nineteenth century, when canals
were dug to drain the marshes, and jetties were built to con-
fine the flow of the Panuco out into the Gulf. These canals
connected three large lagoons, Pueblo Viejo, Chairel and

139

Tamiahua, with the Panuco River. The longest of these canals is known as the Chijol and joins the Panuco with the Tamiahua Lagoon—the largest and longest lagoon along the east coast of Mexico. Subsequently another canal was dug from the south end of the Tamiahua Lagoon to the Tuxpam River. By the turn of this century there had been opened up a vast territory, accessible by canoe, barge and power boats, with Tampico as the natural terminus.

Fifty years ago, Tampico was the terminal for two railways, one running north to Victoria and Monterrey and the other running west to Valles and San Luis Potosi. However, there were no rail lines out of Tampico to the south, although one had been surveyed and right of way graded for some miles south of the Panuco River. Furthermore, there were no all-weather highways (suitable for carts or wagons) in all the east coast of Mexico. Such was the transport situation in the Tampico-Tuxpam area in 1904 when the famous Dos Bocas gusher oil well blew in on the shores of the Tamiahua Lagoon. Within a few years, there was intense drilling activity between Dos Bocas and Rio Tuxpam and many oil fields were developed along a narrow arc-like belt. This belt later became known as the Golden Lane and was generally referred to as being in the South Country (meaning south of Tampico).

You may rightly wonder what all this preamble has to do with walking on fish. By way of reply, I may say that this tale has no point to those who do not comprehend the location and importance of the Chijol Canal. The Chijol was then the only route available for transportation of heavy material and general freight from the Port of Tampico to the South Country. In those days this canal had a depth of about 6 feet, an average width of 30 feet, and extended over a distance of about 8 miles. During the great Golden Lane oil boom of 1905-1925 the Chijol Canal floated a never-ending flotilla of shallow water craft to and fro, day in and day out. Any stoppage in this flow of water traffic could be, and usually was, a matter of great moment.

The following Chijol incident happened during my residence in Mexico (1912-1922) but I do not now recollect the exact year.

I had been down in the South Country on oil company business and was returning to Tampico with several other Americans. We were on board a rather large launch, complete with galley, berths and easy chairs. The weather was clear with little or no wind. The waters of Tamiahua were smooth and sparkling. In every particular our voyage had been pleasant. We were nearing the southern end of the Chijol Canal when the Mexican pilot observed an ever-increasing number of floating fish. Soon all the passengers, as well as the crew, were standing along the sides of our craft to see this strange sight. Literally millions of fish, all kinds and all sizes, lay floating in the Tamiahua waters near the entrance to the canal. All were obviously as dead as the proverbial mackerel. We didn't know what had happened. However, after reducing speed somewhat, we continued on our way into the Chijol. There the mass of dead fish became denser. The bodies were so thick that they had not all turned over, belly up. All the fish were apparently headed toward the Tamiahua. With our launch engines at full speed ahead our progress became slower and slower. Finally, about midway through the canal, the mass of fish so completely blocked the waterway that we were brought to a stop.

Natives stood along the canal banks looking in awe at the phenomenon, never before seen in those parts. Looking up and down the canal we could see that other power craft and barges had been immobilized as we were. Slowly, the almost solid mass of fish and boats moved southward with the tide toward the Tamiahua Lagoon. There was nothing we could do about this inexorable pressure but wait either for the tide to turn or get ashore, if and when we could, and get into Tampico overland. We tried poling but to no avail. Our soundings disclosed the fish mass to be almost solid to the bottom of the canal. Literally, fish were packed on fish, like sardines in a can. We could see that, for the most part, these fish were deep-sea species uncommon to the brackish waters of either the lower reaches of the Panuco River or the Tamiahua Lagoon.

It was growing dusk. We did not relish the thought of spending another day in this fish mess for already the sun had aroused unpleasant odors. We contemplated ways and means of getting ashore and were about to try walking on the top of the fish—several around us were as big as tree trunks—when it was noted that our slow movement backward might bring us close to a small wharf on the canal bank. So we waited a bit and floated to within roping distance of the wharf. Friendly natives cast us a line and by poling we squeezed our launch to dock side. Once on shore, we made our way overland to the south bank of the Panuco from where we ferried over to Tampico.

Life around Tampico for the next ten days or so was misery. The stench of dead fish, floating on the rivers and canals and cast up by the waves on the beaches along the Gulf, was awful. The city authorities would not allow the sale of fish in the market, unless alive. Dead fish were hauled out on the river banks and beaches, piled up, and burned with crude oil. It was weeks before the efforts of man, carnivorous beasts and birds, and the tides, had scoured clean the waterways around Tampico. Fortunately, all the precuations taken prevented any pestilence.

What caused this phenomenon? We never knew. It was not "red tide." All agreed the fish were alive as they swam into the Panuco from the Gulf. Generally, it was conceded that some offshore disturbance had caused deep-sea fish life to seek protected waters in such numbers that they suffocated in the close confines of the canals.

While we didn't actually resort to walking on fish to get ashore from our marooned craft in the Chijol Canal, I still believe we could have done so, if necessary.

Of all venemous insects in Mexico, the centipede is the worst. I have more respect for them than tarantulas or scorpions. Around the oil fields and in Tampico the centipedes are generally potent with venom in every one of their fang-like legs.

The Mexican centipede comes in all sizes, from one inch to over a foot long. And they come in all colors from dull brown to brilliant mottled black, red and yellow. They are to be found in old buildings, dank, dark, dirty corners, in crevices of rocks along streams or in half rotten logs or wood. They crawl up outside walls of houses and slither through cracks into the best of homes, lurking in closets and bathrooms or even in old clothes.

Once while we were living in a fourth floor apartment in Tampico, my wife was getting ready for bed when she noticed an eight incher crawling up inside her night dress near her bosom. She hollered for me and gingerly lifted her nightgown out away from her body. As I got to her, she flipped her gown out and down. The centipede fell to the floor and was stomped to death.

Once my wife was bitten on the big toe by a centipede, during the night. Fortunately, the centipede was a small one else the damage could have been serious. It happened on one of those very hot humid nights when even a sheet on the bed seems like too much cover. Evidently, one corner of my wife's bed sheet had been kicked off onto the floor and attracted the centipede by its warmth. The insect must have been comfortable, snuggled down in the bed clothes. However, it protested by hitting with all fanged feet as my wife pulled up the sheet and thrust her foot downward. She immediately knew what had happened and shook out the insect which she promptly slew with her slipper heel. Then I came to the rescue with a razor blade and iodine. To be sure the antidote would be effective, I bound the iodine onto the toe. That was a mistake, as my wife made known to me the next day in no uncertain terms. Because of the iodine burn she limped around for several days while I was in the "dog house" for malpractice of medicine.

The lady in the apartment below us was entertaining a few bridge friends one afternoon when another "centipede incident" took place. She had been carrying a handkerchief in her hand as she tidied up but had laid it down, still balled up, on a living room table as she went out to the kitchen. When she came back to the living room she picked up her handkerchief and, without looking, crushed it in her hand. She got a terrible centipede bite all across her palm. Evidently, when she left the room the insect had smelled or felt the moist warm linen handkerchief and had crawled beneath or inside it. When the lady of the house closed her hand on the hanky the centipede let go with all his many feet. Our friend had a very bad wound. The whole inside of her palm sloughed off finally. Even after the wound healed one could easily see every fang print, as though her palm had been stitched by a surgeon.

While doing geological work for an English company, one of my well driller friends asked me if I would ride with him over to Tlacolulu from Potrero del Llano to retrieve some clothes he had left in one of the bunkhouses some months previously, when drilling operations in that camp were shut down. It was a rainy day and I could not do any field work so was free to go along. Upon our arrival, we rode straight to the bunkhouse. My companion dismounted and disappeared into the canvas-sided palm-roofed building, while I remained in my saddle. The day was dark and chilly in the rain. I had on both a light coat and a rubber poncho, but my friend had come over without a coat and was cold. It was his old wool coat, particularly, that he wanted to recover from the bunkhouse. He was inside only a few moments and then staggered out, white faced, coat in hand. I asked what the matter was. Soon as he could control his emotions he told how he had gone over to his former bunk and there on a peg in the wall hung his coat. He grabbed it off the wall and started to pull it on, but something caused him to pause and shake the coat. Out dropped centipedes—thirteen of them. The family had found very comfortable quarters, quiet, dark and warm, in the armpit of one of the sleeves. Had my friend not shaken his coat and instead pulled it on over his cotton shirt he would have been badly, if not seriously stung by one or more of these full grown centipedes. This incident was a shock to us both.

Ever afterwards, while in Mexico, I shook out every old garment and every shoe before putting it on.

So far as I know centipedes will not attack anyone. But they do like dark, damp, warm places and they resist being crushed whether intentionally or not. Both my wife and I have learned from experience that it is wise to treat the Mexican centipede with respect.

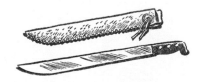

In Mexico, wherever there are cattle there are ticks—or so it was fifty years ago. Mexican cattle ticks come in three sizes, the *pin-a-lea* of pinhead size, the *garr-a-pata* about the size of the blunt end of a pencil and the *con-chuga* which can be as big as a small plum. (These Spanish names are phonetically spelled.)

If one has occasion to ride or walk through a pasture or along a cattle trail in the woods, any part of the body or clothing which brushes the grass or shrubs along the way is sure to be covered with ticks. Some can be readily brushed off, but some are bound to hide in one's breeches, leggings, socks or boots. Those that hide feel or smell the warm flesh and they plunge their spade-like little heads into it and feed off the blood, using their tiny crab-like legs to push the head deep into the flesh. Once attached to the body, they cling and feed for hours and sometimes for days.

When many pin-a-leas get a good hold on a human body the flesh becomes irritated and sometimes mild fever results. Their bodies are so small that it is almost impossible to remove them by hand picking. Our favorite remedy was to apply alcohol in which tobacco leaves had been soaked. However, these tiny mites have a habit of seeking out places where the victim cannot see to remove them. The human eyelids, ears, and behind quarters are particularly vulnerable. Occasionally a tropical sore results.

The larger garr-a-pata is easier to remove. However, hand plucking can be dangerous if care is not taken to remove the tick's head as well as the body. If the head is left in the flesh, a tropical sore is likely. The safest method of removal is to touch the rear end of the tick with a lighted cigarette. This causes the tick to back out quickly and usually it then falls off.

Although I am not versed in insect lore, I believe conchugas are the female of the species. They become attached to the body in some inaccessible place when about garr-a-pata size and gradually grow larger with young. Their body swells like a tiny balloon and when the sack bursts, out pop hundreds of pin-a-leas, raring for red meat. Weeks after leaving the trails, I've found one or more con-chugas on my body, big as marbles. It makes one shudder to remove the pests.

Cattle and wood ticks are the geologists' curse.

Around pigs in Mexico, a fly is commonly found which lays its eggs under the toenail or on the ball of the foot of a sleeping person. This can and does happen frequently when a geologist or engineer sleeps out of doors on a cot beneath a galero—the pigs love to rub their backs against the bottoms of the cots and against the bare feet of the sleeper.

The sleeper is not aware he's being bitten by the fly—there is no pain and no itch. However, if the fly has been successful in laying her hatch, within a few days the infected part becomes sore and swollen. The egg sack lays just below the inner skin and can be seen if one scrapes away the outer layer. The tiny black eggs look like pepper. To remove the egg sack, the field man carefully slits the skin with a razor blade just enough to get at the egg sack, which can easily be removed intact without drawing blood.

If the egg sack develops under a toenail the operation to remove it is more difficult and should be done by a physician, if possible.

Should the egg sack not be removed from the body in time, the eggs become tiny grub-like worms which continue to live in the flesh until removed. I knew one chap who thought it smart to harbor one of these worms in his arm until it got to such heroic size—several inches long—that he had to have it cut out. One way to get rid of such worms is to bind tobacco leaves soaked in aguardiente over the sore; the worm turns to surface for air and dies from the tobacco. The dead worm must be carefully removed intact or a bad sore will result.

The forest and damp lowlands of the sub-tropics are teeming with ants of all kinds, sizes and colors. It is said that ants educate their young, separate themselves into workers, soldiers, kings and queens, go to war, make slaves, keep cows and attend to their toilets, play games, build cemeteries and fortify their dwellings.

The two most interesting varieties commonly encountered by the trail rider in Mexico are the leaf carrying ant and the army ant.

The leaf carriers form an endless procession of leaves coming down from tall trees and stretching out across the forest floor along a path several inches wide. Burden bearers march on one side and workers returning for another load on the other. The cut leaves look like huge sails all out of proportion to the ant's body. One can see the leaves walking but has to look twice to see the carrier. Should a breeze topple over the leaf, an empty handed worker ant quickly assists his brother carrier to reload and carry on. The same assist takes place if the carrier meets some obstacle along the path. It's all well organized and precise, with policemen along the route to keep order and nurses to care for the injured.

Once in a while whole colonies of woods' ants go on the march with a show of martial ardor and discipline that seems almost human. When the ant march is on, all other insects and small creatures get out of their way. The ant army evidently has officers to order its movement, patrols and first aid crews. It proceeds inexorably uphill and down dale, never deviating from the line of march. Should the army meet an obstacle or even a house it goes up and over or through or under but never around. These ants are large and can bite furiously.

I was in a camp once when the army ants came through—literally through my room—by the hundreds of thousands in a line at least two feet across. Cockroaches, mice, scorpions and centipedes rushed out of their path. When a fellow gets army ants in his pants he wastes no time in getting out of those pants, regardless of where he may be at the time.

Wasps usually can be avoided. However, I happened to be along one day when a wasp knocked a fellow geologist (Ben C. Belt*) out cold so quickly that he fell off his horse as though he had been hit by a bullet.

---

*Then, Chief Geologist for Mexican Gulf Oil Company and later, Vice-President of Gulf Oil Corporation.

We were riding a trail along a stretch of country where many bandit raids had been reported. The countryside was brush covered, but dry and almost deserted of population. Ben was just ahead of me as we rode along single file with one mounted mozo leading and another bringing up the rear. At the moment we were silent, listening for we knew not what. The dim trail led us close to a clump of small trees, whose branches hung too low to ride under without ducking our heads.

I saw Ben duck his head and then sway and fall out of his saddle face down. It looked as though he had been shot, but we had heard no shot. Quickly, the two mozos and I dismounted and ran to our companion's side. He was out cold. We looked for a bullet wound and there was none. His heart was beating strongly, so it was not a heart attack. As we bathed his head with water from our canteens, I noticed two small puncture-like wounds at the base of his brain. I called the mozos' attention to these tiny holes and immediately they said "Wasps." Sure enough, we looked back up on the bough under which my friend had ducked and there was a small pear-shaped paper wasp nest. Evidently, papa and mama wasp had been on the outside of their nest as Ben's head came in contact with them, and they both had let him have it right at the base of the brain. The effect was sudden but not lasting. Within a half hour my friend was up and ready to go though he didn't know what had happened until we told him.

In Mexico there is a variety of bees which builds a small paperlike nest on low shrubs.

Once while riding along the trail, I saw my mozo dismount, go over to a bush, shoo off several insects and then tear off a small nest and munch on it as though it were candy. I was intrigued and asked to see what he was eating. He showed me the nest. Broken open it disclosed a score of cells, each containing a drop of honey or an egg sack or a small grub-like bee. My mozo assured me it was *muy dulce* (very sweet) and urged me to try it. Since I couldn't face the grubs I closed my eyes and bit off a hunk of the nest. It was really very good eating—sweet honey flavor, with a hint of juicy meat and wax-like taste of combs.

Mala Mujer means bad woman. It is the name given by the Mexican peon to a plant which in size and leaf somewhat resembles the castor bean plant. Unlike the castor bean, the stalks and leaves of the mala mujer are covered with hair-like spines which sting like nettles. Making one's way through a clump of mala mujer on foot can be very painful.

In the Tierra Caliente of Mexico, mosquitoes and gnats seem to be everywhere, especially around the lagoons along the east coast and the great river systems emptying into the Gulf of Mexico. They attack by night and by day. Years ago they were real pests and malaria was prevalent wherever mosquitoes abounded.

In the Isthmus de Tehuantepec it was too hot and humid to wear gloves and a head cloth, so the geologist fortified himself against the inevitable malaria (*calenturas*) with a daily portion of quinine and wine.

Few Americans develop immunity to malaria although the habitual tobacco user seems to be less vulnerable than the non-user. Most Mexicans have calenturas at infrequent intervals although some of them appear to be immune.

It was because so many Mexicans were chock-full of malaria that the flu epidemic of 1917-1918 took off thousands in the Tampico area alone. The Panuco River floods preceded the epidemic. Many hundreds of poor families fled to the relatively high lands in the city from their wretched homes along the margins of the rivers and lagoons. For days they sat around or walked the streets without shelter and with only meager food. Then came the flu. The flood victims literally died like flies. Hundreds of bodies were carted to the cemetery each dawn. Mothers carried out their little dead babies in wooden wash trays on their heads. Men carried out adults lashed to poles, carried on their shoulders. Some bodies were individually removed by relatives in a sort of stretcher over which temporary awning cover had been arranged. But the bulk were loaded like cordwood onto two wheeled carts over which a loose tarpaulin would be thrown. So many died in such a short time that the bodies could not be buried fast enough to avoid deterioration; therefore, the human bodies were thrown into great heaps, and burned.

Common malaria sometimes runs into intermittent fever or chronic malaria. Black water fever, usually fatal in my day in Mexico, was believed to be a form of malaria. Modern drugs have done much to alleviate the effects of malaria but as long as there is stagnant water in the hot countries, the mosquito will breed and the female will carry the germs from one malaria infested human to another.

An even worst pest is the almost invisible gnat. So small that it can easily pass through an ordinary mosquito netting, this little beast bites with a sting like a bee and draws blood to the surface of the skin. After a day's work in the tropics, one's bare arms, face and neck are freckled with tiny blood clots. Fortunately, smoke or a light breeze will rid the area of these gnats, at least for a time. Wearing muslin over the arms, face and neck will also ward them off. However, in the Isthmus country the weather is usually too hot and humid for this sort of protection. These gnats are a great nuisance, but, as far as I know their bite does not cause fever or any lasting damage to humans.

12

Bandits, Guerrillas,
and Rebels

For ten years after the ousting of Porfirio Diaz in
1910, revolution raged over Mexico. In rapid
succession, the followers of Madero, Huerta, Obregon, Carranza, Zapata, Villa and Palaez took to the field with armed
forces. All these factions were Rebels at first. However, some
were successful in overthrowing the central government and
so became Federalistas while others remained Rebels to the
bitter end. More often than not, the peaceful citizen had no
way of knowing whether attackers were government soldiers
or Rebels; thus, to play safe, when challenged with a "Quien
Vive!," the traveler would usually reply, "Un amigo" (a
friend). The Rebel of that day could be, and often was, the
Federal of tomorrow.

Then, in 1914, World War I began. Many Mexicans were
German sympathizers and soon Mexico was the hottest bed

of international intrigue in all the Americas. When the United States entered the war in 1917, criminals and draft dodgers readily found asylum south of the Rio Grande. This potpourri of anti-social elements produced internal chaos. The malcontents and adventurers who abhorred law and order turned bandits. Such groups roved the countryside between the Rebel and Federal forces, pillaging haciendas, villages, mining camps, oil field camps, and all travelers who were believed to have any valuable goods or money. In the oil field area, some of these bandit groups were directed by Amercian renegades.

Because of the political, social and economic turmoil, Mexican currency became virtually worthless. In the oil fields, workers would accept only gold and silver coin or American dollars in payment for their labor. Payday in the remote oil camps became a recurring headache for management. How to get payrolls safely through the bandit infested countryside was a problem and a risky business.

All sorts of devious ways of transporting payrolls from terminal to camp were resorted to by the oil companies to foil the bandits. Coin was packed in kegs of red lead, in cylinder heads of oil field pumps, in bales of cotton waste, in pipe, in stoves and in any available heavy container being shipped to the fields on barges. Payrolls were carried by speed boats, sometimes in gasoline drums and sometimes concealed in bilge water beneath the floor boards; payrolls were sent overland by car in heavy tool boxes or packed in tires, and occasionally bills and coins were transported in packs on burro backs or in saddle bags by horsemen. In due course, the bandits got wise to all these tricks and consequently, the risks became increasingly greater.

Paymasters, even ex-Texas Rangers imported from the States, did not stay long on the job. They were either killed from bandit ambush or wounded so badly that they quit. Finally, the oil companies resorted to staff volunteers to carry the weekly payroll from Tampico to the oil camps. The same volunteer did not carry the payroll twice in succession and the means of transport and the route were changed each time. Usually, the volunteers were camp bosses and superintendents who frequently had occasion to move in and out of the oil fields on regular business. They were the least suspect. But after a serious holdup, especially if some company employee was killed or wounded, staff volunteers to carry the next payroll were scarce as hen's teeth. Then it was up to management to carry the payroll or else lose face.

Marion Brock, assistant to the vice president in charge of my company's operations in the Texas-Louisiana-Mexico area, had come to Tampico to visit my office and our oil camps in Panuco and the South Country. Naturally, since Brock was considered fair game as a VIP, he was locally conditioned for his field trips by being told all the harrowing tales of banditry and revolution that my associates could muster. For the most part, these stories were true though, no doubt, the facts were elaborated upon with some ghastly details. It was assumed that with this background, Brock would be more appreciative of the trials and tribulations of his associates—at any rate such tales should make his journey into the hinterland more interesting and exciting.

I was to accompany our visitor to the South Country— just the two of us, in an old Ford car—down the Mexican

Gulf Oil Company's pipeline right of way from the south bank of the Panuco River to Toteco, by way of Tepetate, Los Naranjos and Zacamixtle, a distance of about 75 miles. As far as Tepetate, the ride would be rough since the road had been stumped only for single car travel and most of the bridges were the two-plank trestle type. One must keep to the single track or risk tearing out the bottom of the car on a concealed stump or falling off a trestle. For the most part, the trail passed through woodland and bush, which was excellent cover for an ambush.

En route to the ferry across the Panuco, I received word that a bandit party was believed to be operating in the vicinity of Horconcitas, our midway pump station. Accordingly, I was warned to be on the lookout for suspicious characters. Brock felt we should not go but since rumors of that sort were always prevalent, I persuaded him to continue as planned. So, as soon as we were landed on the south bank, we were off, bumpity-bump, at about 25 miles an hour.

We saw no one and heard nothing until we were in sight of Horconcitas. Then, suddenly, another Ford turned onto the right of way from the station clearing and headed in our direction. As it came abreast, I recognized the occupant as our pump station foreman. I asked him if there had been any trouble. He replied, "Not yet, but I came to tell you that a band of about twenty armed men are now at camp looking for the Tampico jefe they say is coming this way. They want to get hold of him for ransom." This was rather alarming. In answer to my further queries, the foreman said the band appeared sober but were well-armed and well-mounted. When he left camp, ostensibly to go to the pump station along the right of way, the bandits were drinking and eating in the mess hall.

Since there were no cut-off auto roads either to the west

or east we must return to Tampico the way we had come
or else proceed down the right of way toward Tepetate,
passing by the pump station. Brock counseled that we go
back, saying that the general agent should not risk capture
for the sake of the company. In as much as our business in
the South Country was not urgent, I was tempted to follow
his advice but on the other hand, one doesn't like to appear
a quitter, especially to a VIP. I asked the foreman if he
thought we had a chance of running by the camp clearing
without being noticed and, if noticed, could we get out of
rifle range before the bandits could fire any telling shots.
He thought we could. Whereupon I told him to return to
the station clearing, with the understanding that if he turned
in toward camp we would know the bandits were still around
the mess hall and it would be reasonably safe for us to drive
on. However, should he continue straight on to the pump
station, it would be a sign to us that the bandits were
gathering there. Then we would decide whether to turn back
or risk being shot at, if we went on. It was agreed. As the
foreman headed away from us, Brock again tried to convince
me that, after all, it really wasn't important that he see the
South Country. I turned a deaf ear, with much more bravo
externally than I felt in my insides.

As the foreman neared the clearing we got set, with the car
motor idling. Without stopping, the foreman turned in toward
the camp and disappeared from view behind the trees. With
shaking knees, I pressed the accelerator all the way to the floor
boards. Our car jumped forward and hurtled down the rough
trail with us hanging on for dear life. Brock was trying to
whistle up his courage—his side of the car was nearest the
clearing—but no sound came forth, only wind from his
puckered lips. As we bounced and rocked ahead, I was silently
praying that the motor would not break down or that we'd not
have a tire puncture, at least until we were well out of bandit
range.

Evidently, the bandits heard our car before they sighted us, for, as we came abreast of the clearing, we could see men grabbing up rifles and running to their horses. A few wild shots were fired before we disappeared down the right of way and out of rifle range. We kept going for several miles before stopping to survey what damage, if any, we had suffered. There was no sign of pursuit. Neither we nor the car had been hit, but both Brock and I were wet with nervous perspiration and our backsides were lame from the bouncing we'd taken on our wild ride. Brock was still whistling, more audibly now that the immediate danger was over.

Without further incident of consequence, we proceeded on our way to Tepetate. There, I phoned back to the Horconcitas foreman for information as to what had happened at his end after our escape. He told me that for a few minutes all hell broke loose. The bandits were upset and angry over losing a hostage and threatened to kill everyone at camp. However, after cursing for a while and firing some shots through the buildings, they rode off, vowing vengeance. "Under the circumstances," the foreman said, "you and your Houston friend had better not return through Horconcitas." I thanked him for making it possible for us to get safely away and assured him that we would motor back to Tampico along some other pipeline route. (That foreman was the real hero of this incident.)

We tarried in and around the oil field camps for several days before setting out on our return. Meanwhile, I had had the Ford thoroughly overhauled as insurance against any ordinary breakdown on the road. We decided to follow the Huasteca pipelines on the homeward trek, as a fairly decent road had been graded and was maintained along that route. Although the distance would be longer that way, we should be able to make better time.

All went well until we got a few miles south of the Huasteca Oil Company's Horconcitas pump station, some miles east of our company's station of the same name. All of a sudden, as we rounded a curve in the woods, we ran smack-dab into a mounted band riding toward us. We were quickly halted at gunpoint and surrounded. They were obviously a Rebel group —fortunately sober—and probably the same band that had tried to capture us a few days ago. We could see that they had a Mexican haciendado trussed up on one of the lead horses, most likely a hostage. In answer to their questions, I lied about our business, our company affiliations, and where we had been or were going. Finally, they were convinced that we were only young Americans, of no official importance, going to Tampico to have a good time down the line. And so, were allowed to continue on our way unmolested.

Had this group been drunk or had they not found another hostage, Brock and I might not have escaped so easily.

The Maumee River is a small branch of the Rio Tancho-chin which empties into the Tamiahua Lagoon. It is navigable for shallow draught craft for a short distance up from its mouth. It was on this stream that my company built a dock for unloading material and oil field equipment brought down by barges from Tampico. From this water terminal, material intended for Tepetate and the other oil camps further south was trucked overland on a well-graded oiled road bed.

The Maumee terminal marked our pipeline crossing. An auto ferry was maintained there for the convenience of employees traveling to and from Tampico and the South Country. This ferry was a two-car or one-truck job, operated by a cable stretched across the stream. At either end it had aprons which could be raised and lowered by ropes to admit and discharge vehicles. The river banks on both sides were fairly steep in spite of having been cut back on a slope from the water's edge. During times of low waters, cars were known to be stuck on the ferry for hours because the river bank grade was too great for the cars to cope with, even in low gear.

During one season of low water I had made an auto trip from Tampico to the oil fields in the South Country. I was traveling alone in an old but well serviced Ford. Outbound, I had no unusual difficulty crossing the Maumee on the ferry. But while I was in the field it rained—not enough to swell the streams but more than enough to make unoiled, non-graded roads a morass of mud.

Normally, the run from Maumee to the Panuco River took two or three hours and it was with this in mind that I delayed my departure from Tepetate until early one afternoon. When I got to the ferry, the Mexican in charge said, "I wouldn't try to cross now, if I were you, because the water is very low, the opposite bank is very muddy and just out of view on the other side is a group of bandits drinking at a cantina." The ferry-man went on to explain that the cantina was set about 20 yards back in the brush from the pipeline right of way, but facing the road, with a considerable clearing in front. Accord-ing to the ferryman, the bandits were now well-liquored up and were getting rowdy and even fighting among themselves. In their present condition they were not a crowd that a lone American would care to mingle with.

In answer to my inquiry, the ferry man said we could prob-ably cross on the ferry to the other side without the bandits hearing us, and that we would not be in their view unless they rode down to the river bank. But getting off the barge would be a real problem and, he added, "the bandits will certainly hear your car, as you rev up the motor to take the steep grade, then you can expect them to come on the run."

It was not a pleasant prospect, but I wanted to get home by nightfall, if possible. At least I would cross to the other side and have a look and then decide whether to risk the run or not. Every now and then we heard the sound of shots from the cantina, indicating that a free-for-all fight might be in the making. With some trepidation, I braked my car down the slope onto the ferry, with the motor cut off. As the ferry eased away from shore, I allowed the car to slide back on the barge as far as the rear apron, thus tipping the forward end up. On reaching the opposite bank, the ferryman hauled the barge as far up the slope as it would go before silently lower-ing the apron at that end. Even so the slope was steep and formidable with mud. When the ferry had been made fast by ropes to stakes on shore, I started my motor, pushed the pedal in low gear and gave my Ford the gun. The traction on the ferry was fairly good, but I barely made the top of the slope even with my foot pressing the accelerator down to the floor. My knees were shaking so much I feared my foot would slip off the accelerator.

By the time I had got up to the road level I could see the bandits running for their horses and making in my direction, shouting and shooting. The Ford was quivering and laboring. I was too, for that matter. Fortunately, the motor had a quick pick-up and soon it was in high, going hell bent across the clearing. Those trigger happy drunken bandits did a powerful lot of shooting but fortunately for me, neither the car nor I were hit.

It was just another incident in a day's work in the oil fields of Mexico.

John Eads, the Mexican Gulf Oil Company's current paymaster, was an old-time settler in Mexico. He knew the country in and around the oil fields like a book, and was no novice to the bandit situation. For some months he was able to carry the payrolls to the several oil camps on time and without serious trouble. From time to time he varied his mode of travel and his schedule. Both were kept secret until he was well on his way.

We had heard rumors of a group of bandits, said to be head-quartered somewhere near Topila. This band had been seen once or twice in the vicinity of our Horconcitas pump station but mostly they operated in the Topila-Panuco oil field area. For some time now they had laid low, so there was hope that they had either disbanded or moved on out of the region. Thus, it seemed reasonably safe to carry the next payroll overland down the pipeline route.

That payroll was about $30,000, all in American dollars and Mexican silver coin. Because of the silver, the payroll would be heavy and bulk large. So, for this trip, John Eads arranged to use a light Ford truck and took along a trustworthy Texas-Mexican lad for driver. John was armed with pistol and shotgun but the boy carried only a knife. John had instructed his driver that, in the event of an ambush, he was to make his getaway if possible through the monte and under no circumstances to stand and fight.

They started out one day shortly before noon. About fifteen miles south of the Panuco River in brush country they ran into a volley of rifle shots; one bullet hit John in the knee and another struck him in the shoulder. Armed men appeared in the right of way ahead and on the Topila side. John called to his driver that he was hurt badly, to turn the car into the monte and to jump out and make his way back for help. In his wounded condition, John could not put up a fight, and it would have been useless if he had. The bandits swarmed around, quickly found the loot, kicked John a few times, snatched his guns, and then made off into the brush.

John managed to lie down in the shade alongside his car and bind his wounds enough to stop the bleeding. He could do nothing more then, but rest quietly and wait for help. It was nearly nightfall when the heavily armed rescue party arrived with cot, blankets and first aid kits. Horconcitas pump station had phoned in to the Prieto Terminal office that the paymaster had not passed there on schedule, so the terminal was alerted for trouble even before John's driver had made his way overland afoot. Soon as the lad had got his breath and a bite to eat, he took off with the rescue party to guide them to the scene of the ambush.

At the hospital the doctors said John's shoulder wound was not serious, however, the knee injury was bad and might lame him for life. He was able to walk only with the aid of a cane for many years afterwards.

Our field staff was very much upset by this incident. It was generally felt that something must be done to make travel safe down the company's pipeline right of way. Ambuscades must cease. The bandits must be taught a lesson they'd never forget. But how and who would do it? We couldn't count on either Federal or Rebel troops to catch or scatter the bandits because kith and kin from both sides were mixed up with the marauders. As we expected, the Federal troops, sent out to the scene of the attack on Eads, reported that the bandits had escaped, leaving no trail.

Finally, two of my men decided to take matters into their own hands. Both were superintendents—one of pipelines and the other of production—and both were Texans with reputations for being able to handle any kind of gun. (For our story, I shall refer to my friends only as Pete and Jim.) Word got to me in Tampico that these fellows were going on a secret two-man crusade. I phoned through to Pete for confirmation and details. He said, "Boss forget it—the less you know the better—but we'll give you the details if and when we get back." I tried to argue against taking the law into their own hands, but Pete said, "To hell with the law that permits our friends to be shot from ambush without warning," and hung up on me.

A few days later, Pete and Jim told me that their venture

had been most successful with nobody hurt, except four or five bandits who would not be bothering anyone again on this earth. It seems that they had enlisted John Ead's Tex-Mex lad to drive a lead car, with Pete and Jim following some 100 yards behind in a second car. The plan was to follow Eads' route, the two cars keeping in sight of one another, but well apart. The Tex-Mex lad was told to drive into the monte on his left at the sight of any armed man or the sound of a rifle shot and then to jump out and beat it, leaving Pete and Jim in the car behind to take care of the situation.

In anticipation of this venture word had "leaked" that our company was sending another payroll to the South Country to replace the stolen one. (This I didn't know either until afterwards.) On the scheduled departure for the false payroll movement, the two cars took off. Nothing happened until they got near the site of Eads' ambush. Then suddenly, Pete and Jim heard a rifle shot and saw the Tex-Mex turn his car into the monte and jump out. Immediately they turned to the opposite side of the road and leaped into the monte with their sawed off shotguns and side arms. They could see the bandits swarming over the decoy car, virtually tearing it to pieces looking for loot. When nothing of value was found, one of the bandits discovered the second car down the road. They all came running and shouting and shooting. Pete and Jim waited silently until the gang came into close range before they opened up on belly targets, with both pistol and shotgun. Four bandits fell mortally wounded, while a fifth made off, bleeding profusely, with the aid of the rest of the gang. Soon all was quiet again. Pete and Jim reconnoitered and found the surviving bandits had all escaped. They called to the Tex-Mex lad, who came out of hiding, unhurt. A hurried examination disclosed that both cars would still run, although the body of the lead car had been battered, the tool box smashed open and the spare tire cut to ribbons. The cars were turned around and arrived back in town before nightfall.

The bodies of the dead bandits were left on the right of way where they had fallen and there they remained for days until sun, beast and buzzard had removed all signs of conflict.

No account of this incident ever appeared in the press, but by the grapevine everyone in the oil fields knew what had happened and who had done it. There was no official inquiry. And what is more important, there were no more bandit ambuscades along that stretch of road.

This ambush in reverse brought relative peace and quiet.

During the lull which followed the John Eads incident and the reprisal, it was necessary for an official of the Mexican Gulf Oil Company to proceed to the South Country in order to sign certain lease papers and, coincidently, pay over a substantial cash sum. Accordingly, as general agent, I prepared for the trip. Since there had been no bandit trouble for some time, I decided to go alone by car down the pipe-line right of way.

With my papers and money thrown loosely in an old burlap sack, I took a launch from Tampico and rode up to the company's tanker loading terminal in Prieto, where a car had been made ready. The terminal superintendent, Norman Perry, met me and advised that my car was already on the barge used for ferrying our vehicles across the Panuco River. I noted he was not only wearing side arms, as I was, but carried a shotgun. When I asked where he was going, Norman said, "Jefe, I'm going with you for company. Besides, I've also got business in the fields." I was glad for his company and told him so. I knew Norman was a quiet sort of follow until aroused; then he was a whirlwind of words and action. He was one of the few two-gun men I had ever come across in the oil country.

In due course, we were rolling down the highway in a stripped-down Ford runabout with windshield down and no top. I was driving. As we took off, Norman said, "Jefe, we will be passing the scene of Eads' ambush and while there has been no recent bandit trouble hereabouts, we'd better plan what to do and how to do it, if we're attacked." When I asked Norman if he had a plan in mind he said, "Yes, in the unlikely event we should see any armed person step out of the monte ahead or if we should hear a rifle shot you drive the car quickly off the right hand side of the road and into the brush, where we can both jump out and conceal ourselves until we can reconnoiter the situation." Remembering Eads' incident and the reprisal, I at once agreed.

Our pipeline right of way crossed a number of small streams and bayous, over which low wooden bridges and trestles had been built. These were mostly makeshift structures without side rails and often with loose floor boards. On the trestles the floor boards were laid parallel to the car wheels, one plank wide on each side. Under such circumstances, it was advisable to slow down at every water crossing and to proceed over with caution.

It was a beautiful day. We laughed and joked and generally felt gay, until we neared the place of former ambuscade. Then we both tensed and grew silent. Norman remarked that the place where the reprisal had occurred lay just ahead "over yonder bridge." I slowed down for the narrow bridge and was almost over the planking when we heard the sound of a rifle shot close at hand. Quickly, I accelerated the old Ford, turned off the road into the monte and cut the motor as we both jumped for cover. I grabbed my Colt 45 automatic from the holster and held it ready as I crouched behind a sizeable tree. Norman, his shotgun in one hand and a pistol in the other, also crouched behind a tree. We heard no further shots or any suspicious noises. Up and down the right of way we looked—nobody could be seen. Then it dawned on us what had happened. Rather foolishly, we both looked out at our car and, sure enough, we saw that a rear tire had blown. Happening as it had over water, the blow-out had sounded exactly like a 30-30 rifle.

My heart was still thumping madly as we came out of the woods to make repairs and continue our journey southward. Norman had remained cool and calm through it all, but then, he was a Texan.

During the period 1916-1920 in Mexico, Federalistas controlled the tanker loading terminals at Tampico and Tuxpam while the Rebel forces controlled the major oil fields of northern Veracruz. The oil companies paid export and other taxes to the central government and also paid tribute to the Rebels. Since oil must be produced before it could be refined for local consumption or exported as crude, the Federal government condoned the payment of tribute to the Rebels; in fact, the oil companies were allowed to deduct the tribute from their taxes.

Now the company with which I was then associated had substantial oil production in the South Country, which was moved by pipeline to Tampico and then loaded onto tankers. In order to produce, my company was required to pay a monthly tribute of 3,000 pesos (then about $1600) in American bills or Mexican coins. We were instructed to deliver this in the South Country to Col Rabité, an officer in the Rebel army under General Manuel Palaez. Customarily, our monthly tribute was carried to the Rebels by staff volunteers such as the drilling or pipeline superintendent, the camp cashiers or camp bosses. The payments when made were recorded on the company's financial records and "expensed" to the head office.

In between the Federalists and Rebels were roving bandits who preyed on those carrying payrolls and tribute. They shot from ambush, indiscriminantly. They held up cars on the road and waylaid barges and launches. Life was hectic. The tribute must get through yet it was as much as one's life was worth to carry money on the trail.

As general manager, it was my responsibility to arrange for these monthly payments and to render an expense account of the tribute money. We called it "Extraordinary Expense for the month of————." This went on for some months until one day Tampico was instructed by the head office to render receipts with such expense accounts. Promptly I advised all concerned to obtain receipts. But no receipts were forthcoming. So, to set an example, I told the staff that I would carry the tribute money to the Rebel forces, and I would get a receipt or know the reason why.

Accordingly, I packed the monthly tribute in a shoe box and started out by car for Zacamixitle, some 75 miles south of Tampico. I managed to evade the bandits and eventually got through to Zacamixitle, an Indian town and an oil field of sorts lying between Los Naranjos and Cerro Azul. There,

I inquired for Col. Rabité. I was told he was nearby in his monte retreat and a guide was assigned to escort me to him.

Col. Rabité was a Mexican of French descent probably stemming from Maximilian's time. He was a tall, fair-haired man with steel blue eyes, reputedly cold-blooded and cruel. Some folks said he was loco. I knew for a fact that Col. Rabité had commandeered one of my company's launches for use as a makeshift flagship on the Tamiahua Lagoon, and while cruising on that boat, he had wantonly stabbed our Chinese cook in the back and pushed him overboard simply because the Chinese boy didn't bring him his coffee fast enough. This was only one of many crazy acts of this trusted emissary of General Palaez. Knowing these gruesome stories of Rabité, I was apprehensive of his reception. Still I had a job to do so I got on with it.

I was blindfolded in Zacamixitle and led along devious trails through the woods to a clearing. There my guide removed the blindfold and shoved me toward a palm-thatched hut. The guard at the hut threw his 30-30 rifle down on me and challenged me with, "Quien Vive?." He was a mean looking fellow with side arms and a knife as well as the rifle. I replied, "Un amigo de Colonel Rabité." The guard dropped the point of his gun and motioned me forward. Clutching my package of money I advanced to the hut. Just inside the door was a chair and table—in the chair sat Col. Rabité. I saluted, told my name, and said I had come for my company with this month's payment for General Palaez. He got up, all six feet of him, faced me with hands on hips, and stared with his cold blue eyes. Finally Rabité said, "Give it to me."

I handed over the money pack and said, "My company wants a receipt for this payment."

He laid the package on the table unopened, glared at me for a moment and then dropped his hand onto the butt of his pistol and said in Spanish, "Here is your receipt. Do you want it?" Naturally, I didn't want a bullet—only a piece of paper—and yet I knew from his attitude and reputation that the crazy colonel would as soon shoot me as he would a stray dog. Under such circumstances I didn't argue, but politely said I would forget the receipt and left as quickly as possible.

Upon returning to Tampico, I wrote the auditors in our head office that if the records of tribute money paid to the Rebels could be satisfied only by written receipts, they had better send someone along capable of obtaining same—we couldn't, and we would not risk trying again.

We heard nothing further from the head office about receipts.

I never knew Monty Michael, but his name, reputation and exploits were legend during the early years in the Mexican oil fields. He appeared on the scene shortly before the United States entered World War I. Some said he was wanted in the States on criminal charges, others said he was a draft dodger, but all agreed that he was a competent oil well driller and a hard man.

After coming to Mexico he drifted from one company to another. His work was satisfactory, but he got into all kinds of trouble with his men and the management. His friends were men of questionable character, mostly roughnecks—good oil men but rowdy off the job. Wherever he worked, oil field equipment disappeared overnight to no one knew where. This went on for a year or more until one day Monte set himself up as drilling contractor with a full complement of tools, rig, boilers and a crew.

One small newcomer company gave him a contract to drill a well on a lease adjoining a lease of one of the larger American oil companies. Shortly after Monty's outfit rigged up, the other company also started an offset well a few hundred feet away. Drilling progressed on both wells, with evident signs of bitter rivalry between the two crews. However, Monty's rig began to have trouble at about 3,000 feet. His boilers leaked steam so badly his fireman could not maintain pressure. Slower and slower went Monty's rig while the other company's offset penetrated deeper and deeper with their new equipment and high pressure boilers.

Now Monty had contracted for a bonus payment if his well came in before the other company's. He wanted, and needed, that bonus to hold his tough gang in line. He tried to make a deal with the other boss driller but failed.

The offset well drilled into the limestone and shut down to rig up the cable tools while Monty's hole was still short of the limestone by several hundred feet. It was customary in those days in Mexico, especially during the rigging stage, for oil well drilling crews to knock off for lunch. So the offset well crew went to lunch at their drilling camp about a half mile from the rig. It was a good lunch and a beastly hot day so the crew took a long hour. When they got back on the job they found that Monty had moved their hot boilers, complete with connections, from their rig to his and was unconcernedly drilling ahead. The outraged crew protested but Monty just stood his ground, with his hands on two six guns and dared them come and take back what he called their abandoned property. He kept those boilers until his hole was completed, and then left them standing for the other company to recover when he moved off.

The law never caught up with Monty for this bold steal; however, it became increasingly difficult for him to get a drilling contract with any reputable company after that incident. He was on the black list.

As far as I know, the stolen hot-boiler episode was Monty's last effort to work at his trade for others. Soon he turned renegade and began to raid and rob with his mixed gang of Americans and Mexicans. He was smart and tough and struck at oil camps and paymasters when least expected. The authorities seemingly could not, or at least did not, have any success in breaking up this strong, well armed, well mounted bandit group. As the gang prospered they grew in numbers and became bolder. It was their success that caused their downfall. The troops were called out and instructed to show no mercy—to shoot to kill. Eventually, Monte and his gang were caught off guard and summarily shot. Monty's body was exhibited to the public in Ebano (an oil field town) and in Tampico to convince the people that this bad man had truly bit the dust.

The Sunday *Post-Dispatch*, May 28, 1922, carried a long and vivid story about this renegade entitled "Monte Michaels, Recently Slain, No Ordinary Bandit"—"Most Spectacular Feat of American in Mexico Was to Squat on Claim, Steal Drill and Strike Oil":

Ebano, State of Vera Cruz, Mexico.—It is no ordinary bandit who is able to lay false claim to a piece of choice oil land, steal a derrick, drilling outfit and all other necessary equipment, put down the well himself and have the luck to bring in a 60,000 barrel producer. That was also one of the many daring and spectacular exploits performed by "Monte" Michaels during his tempestuous career in the oil fields of the gulf coast region of Mexico. He met his death recently on the ranch of E. L. Doheny of Los Angeles, Cal., and associates at the home of the superintendent, Ed Watt, near here. Michaels was attempting to break into the ranch-house for the purpose of robbery when he was shot through the head by Watt.

Although banditry has been more or less rife in Mexico for many years, no native leader of these lawless forces was ever more feared in the territory where he operated than was "Monte" Michaels. At the same time, like most traditionary brigands of the old-time days, he had certain good qualities that won for him the respect and loyalty of the peon or Indian element of the rural districts and the towns, including the city of Tampico, which Michaels was wont to visit occasionally even when a big price was upon his head.

No finer specimen of humanity, physically speaking, ever came to Mexico than "Monte" Michaels. He was 32 years old at the time he was killed. Big, well proportioned, blue-eyed, and with a mop of curly brown hair he was an outstanding figure wherever he went—upon the streets of the city as he strode along or in the oil fields where originally he performed his work as a professional well driller.

Another thing about Michaels was that he took unbounded joy in his work. He always wore a smile. When Watt fired the shot that ended the man's earthly career, Michaels' face wore a broad smile that might have served to mask the stern purpose behind the attempt at house-breaking. That Michaels was looked upon more as a hero than a bandit was shown by the signal honors that were paid him upon his death.

His body was taken to Tampico and placed in a box in front of the city hall where it was viewed by thousands of people. Americans of Tampico, some of them whom Michaels had robbed, raised a purse and he was given a funeral equal to that which any member of the colony there might expect at the hands of its members.

Born in Pennsylvania

Nothing is known here about Michaels' life before he came to the oil fields. As a matter of fact he was so young, only 20 years old, when he turned up in Tampico that he could not have made a very long record of any kind before that. He had worked in the oil fields of Texas before coming to Mexico. He was born in Pennsylvania, he told friends here, but whereabouts in that State, he was never heard to say.

For a time Michaels led a comparatively quiet life in the different oil camps of the Tampico region. Then he began frequenting the cantinas and gambling halls. His favorite game of chance was monte and his success at times in winning considerable sums of money caused him to be given the nick-name of "Monte" Michaels. This name clung to him so close that his real given name was forgotten.

Michaels went from bad to worse. He became envious, it is said, of the remarkable success of big financial interests in playing the oil game in Mexico. He was often heard to declare that he had as much right to a share of the oil as the big companies and he proposed to get it. By this time he was lording it over the oil camps wherever he happened to be. He used his fists and guns freely. The police and rural authorities were afraid of him. Every night or two he would shoot up some native village or go on a rampage that would throw terror into the hearts of the people of the community.

Of the many crimes which are laid at his door none brought Michaels into more disrepute than the blowing up by dynamite of the special train carrying the payroll of the International Petroleum Co. last fall. In the explosion seven persons were killed. Not long after this a detachment of soldiers was led to the mountain rendezvous of the bandits and made an attack upon the Mexicans on guard there. One bandit was killed and a big store of stolen goods recovered. Michaels was absent from the camp at the time.

This American bandit is known to have given money to many poor Mexican families. He often declared that he never robbed anyone but the rich oil companies or their representatives. It had been known for some time that he was in the vicinity of Ebano. He and his band had stolen many cattle from the ranch of Doheny and associates and recently a request was made of the Government to send soldiers to guard the ranch and Ebano. A military force was sent to this place a few days before Michaels came to his end.

Riff-raff and draft dodgers flocked into the oil fields of Mexico from the United States and elsewhere during World War I. Mexico was a haven for the criminal, the radical, the adventurer and cripples. In the oil company offices, the oil fields and the camps any man with clerical ability or a skill could find ready employment with no questions asked as to the applicant's history or the why and wherefor of his seeking work in Mexico. Such was the labor situation all during the United States' participation in the War while I was general agent of the Mexican Gulf Oil Company.

One day, a Lt. Commander in the U. S. Naval Intelligence called on me to say that my company had on its clerical staff at Prieto a criminal character—wanted in the U. S. for murder and other crimes—who was secretary of Mexico's IWW syndicate. The International Workers of the World (IWW) mostly included in its ranks radicals and vicious persons, whose aim was to overthrow any constituted government, by any means. The Lt. Commander suggested that the company rid itself of this hotbrand and arrange, if possible, that he be black-balled from employment by any other oil company in Mexico lest there occur acts of sabotage to wells, pipelines, stations or tanks that might jeopardize the flow of much needed Mexican fuel oil to the world navies.

The alleged IWW secretary was described as being a small, slightly built middle-aged man with blond hair, blue eyes and an inoffensive manner. My informant said this fellow resembled a barber in appearance and manner and would not be recognized as being the ruthless character he really was. Naval Intelligence had ascertained that this man had been known in the States under the alias of Nitokin or Nikolin, was wanted for murder in Arizona, and had been deported from America at one time along with Emma Goldman. I was counseled to rid the company of him quietly and quickly, with the minimum of fuss.

I telephoned through to Prieto and talked with Superintendent Eddie Morend, told him briefly and guardedly about the fellow and asked him to arrange the discharge at once without involving the head office. Eddie said he would carry out my orders, although I sensed he was miffed and perhaps didn't believe what I had been told. He insisted the clerk had performed his duties well and had caused no trouble at all.

The next morning I entered my office shortly after eight as usual. A few moments later, my secretary (an able young man with a wooden leg) came quickly in and, when he reached my side, said in a low voice, "Nitokin or Nikolin—whatever the alleged secretary of Mexico's IWW organization is now known by—is outside and insists on seeing you personally. I think he's got a gun." (I thought to myself, what does one do when confronted by a desperate radical, who, by profession, brooks no obstacle. Frankly, I was scared.) I told my secretary to send the fellow in, but to leave the door ajar and, if he should hear any commotion, to come arunning.

A few moments later Nitokin was ushered in. He looked like his description—a smallish, blond, blue eyed fellow, neatly dressed and mild mannered. At my invitation, he seated himself in an arm chair close to the left hand side of my large, flat top double desk. He hitched his chair almost within my reach before he spoke. Then he said, "You are the general agent of this company, are you not?"

I replied, "Yes."

Then leaning forward with his elbows on my desk, he asked, "Why did you order me fired?"

For a moment I was too nonplused for words. (I thought, why under the sun did Eddie tell this fellow that the head office wanted him fired. Evidently he had been told just that. Now what to do.) I determined to brave the issue as boldly as possible. I dropped my right hand onto the butt of my 45 Colt automatic as it lay hidden from view in the partially opened drawer of my desk and said, "Nitokin, I am told that your work and conduct while with my company have been satisfactory. However, I am informed that you are wanted for murder up north, that you were once deported from the United States and are now secretary to the IWW's in Mexico. My country does not want men of your reputation on its payroll."

He sat and stared at me coldly. I watched his hands closely for any move that might suggest he was going to pull a knife or a gun. We both sat quietly and looked at one another for what seemed like minutes before Nitokin spoke.

Again he leaned forward—our heads almost touching— "Mr. Hamilton," he said, "you will be sorry for what you've done to me." With that he got up and walked out of my office, neither looking back nor saying another word.

As soon as Nitokin was out of the building I reported the incident, as quickly as possible, to all the other oil companies and to my Naval Intelligence friend. I also let off steam to the Prieto superintendent, who had let me down so badly.

I never saw or heard of Nitokin again, except in my nightmares. He disappeared altogether from the oil fields of Mexico, so far as I know. However, I shall never forget those anxious moments as we faced one another across my desk. I guess I was just plumb scared of what a man with Nitokin's reputation might do out of vengeance.

A few nights later someone tried unsuccessfully to break into my Tampico apartment, where I lived with my wife and baby boy, but I never knew if it was Nitokin or someone else. At any rate, nothing came of it.

So the Nitokin incident became just another of the tense events common to those hectic times in Mexico.

The repercussion of World War I and the violent, though spotted, internal revolution created in Mexico an almost total disregard of law and order during 1917 and 1918. Bandits vied with the wandering Rebels in openly terrorizing both country and city. The oil camps were big game for all marauders. More often than not they came unheralded, struck and disappeared into the unknown. What happened at the Mexican Gulf Company's Prieto Terminal, within sight of the city of Tampico, shortly after 1:00 P.M. Saturday, June 29, 1918, was one of many such episodes.

The San Luis Potosi-Tampico Railway bisected the terminal property—the oil loading docks, camp buildings and warehouses being on the river side and the tank farm and pump station lying inland from the railroad. The public moved freely along the terminal river front by boat and pedestrians roamed at will along the tracks. This was the setting of one of the boldest and bloodiest robberies of oil camps in Mexico during my day.

The following account of this raid, even without the gory details, affords a graphic picture of the time and conditions in Mexico:

Five bandits, armed with 30-30 rifles, entered the main section of the Terminal at the western end, and from the railroad track. They made their way to the warehouse, in the front part of which the Cashier's office was located, and found therein L. R. Millard, Assistant Cashier, R. M. Cooper and L. A. Dunn. Millard was complying with their order to turn over to them the money he had when a signal sounded in the Boiler Station. It was intended to summon to the telephone Alfred E. Esparcia, Master Mechanic, an American citizen of Mexican ancestry. Apparently believing this signal indicated that their holdup was about to be repelled, the bandits opened fire on the three men above, killing them, as well as Esparcia, while he was trying to answer the telephone, and Natividad Flores, a Mexican watchman.

The bandits then fled by the way they had come, and tracks were discovered showing they had escaped in a launch or canoe which had been hidden at the bank of the lagoon on the north-side of the railroad track and west of the Terminal, which gave rise to an unconfirmed conjecture that they were residents of the Tamesi River section. Federal soldiers were summoned and took up the search, but, so far as the record shows, none of the bandits was apprehended.

The loot amounted to 9,427.61 Moneda Nacional, or the equivalent of approximately $3,700.00 U. S. Cy.

13

Gunboats and Tankers

During the politically unsettled period in Mexican affairs which followed the resignation of Porfirio Diaz as President of the Republic of Mexico (1910) and the beginning of World War I (1914), naval vessels of many nations were stationed off Veracruz and Tampico as protection to foreigners. In the Panuco River in front of Tampico there were, from time to time, gunboats of Germany, the United States, the Netherlands, the United Kingdom, and France, as well as Mexico. However, with the outbreak of the War in Europe only U.S. naval craft remained to patrol the Gulf ports of Mexico.

In 1916 and early 1917 the U.S.S. *Tacoma* was a familiar sight to Tamipiquenos. Americans, particularly, welcomed the sight of their flag waving from the *Tacoma's* stern during daylight hours, and slept better at night for the knowledge that their marines were standing guard, ready for any emergency. Between the incidents of internal revolution and the European war, the oil port of

Tampico was in almost constant turmoil and ferment with alarms and rumors. On several occasions, American women and children and some men were evacuated by ships to Texas ports. My company, like some other oil companies, kept a yacht almost constantly in Tampico waters ready to evacuate its employees in case of siege or other hazards to life.

Notwithstanding these critical times and circumstances, work in the oil fields continued unabated. Wells were drilled, gushers came in and were controlled, new pipelines and pump stations were built and Mexican oil from the South Country, the Panuco Region and Ebano continued to flow to the world markets through the oil ports of Tuxpam, Lobos, and Tampico. Daily, tankers called at these ports for cargoes of Mexican "liquid gold."

At Port Lobos and Tuxpam there were no sheltered harbors, and the tankers were loaded off shore through submarine pipelines. At Tampico, however, the Panuco River was navigable for loaded tankers drawing up to 25 feet, from the Gulf of Mexico upstream to Prieto, some five miles above the Fiscal Wharf at Tampico.

In those days tankers were small compared with the huge tanker vessels of today. One of the smallest of these oil tankers was the S.S. *Winifred* belonging to the Gulf Refining Company—her maximum cargo capacity was about 20,000 barrels of 12° gravity crude.

Due to the cooperation of the officers and crew of the U.S.S. *Tacoma* early in 1917, the *Winifred* was saved from being lost when it went on the beach, fully loaded, just outside the Panuco River breakwaters. On this occasion the *Winifred* had been loaded at Prieto and hurriedly put to sea before an impending norther broke. The downstream navigation was without incident. The river pilot was put off, as usual, at San Carlos, near the inner end of the stone jetties on either side of the channel. The Gulf of Mexico waters were calm but the sky was ominous. Once the pilot was safely aboard his tender, the *Winifred* resumed speed into the open sea.

Just as the *Winifred* crossed the outer bar, the keel grounded and the ship's bow swung sharply to the starboard around the outer end of the south breakwater. After the grounding, the ship did not respond to her helm (later, it was ascertained the ship's rudder had been carried away) and soon lay broadside to the beach just south of the south breakwater with her beam exposed to the full force of the breakers rolling in from the open Gulf. In this position, an effort was made to anchor the vessel, but the sea parted both chains. In a matter of minutes the tanker had been successively lifted and impelled shoreward over several sand bars, until it lay, canted over, in relatively shallow water, about a half mile off shore.

On board the tanker, the officers and crew worked feverously to lay anchors out from both stern and bow. The groundings had evidently broached the hull, for water flooded the engine room making it necessary to draw the fire from under the boilers. All this time, the sky blackened and the winds began to pick up from the north. Should the storm break in full fury before the tanker could be got off the sand bars into deep water it must surely be lost. Having done everything they could to secure their craft in its helpless condition, the officers and crew came ashore in the vessel's lifeboats.

This incident happened at a time when all tank ships, regardless of size, were needed to carry fuel to and from the United States, even though our country was not yet at war. Naturally, Gulf's office in Tampico and the staff of the U.S.S. *Tacoma* were very much concerned over the possible loss of the *Winifred,* either through being totally wrecked by the impending norther or by being boarded by Germans or Mexicans claiming the abandoned hulk as a prize.

As general agent of the Mexican Gulf Oil Co., I consulted my friends among the officers of the *Tacoma* for advice and aid. It was agreed to send a small detachment of marines onto the beach opposite the *Winifred* and there set up camp to take care of the tanker's crew. Also, the *Winifred's* captain and chief engineer were "invited" to come on board the *Tacoma* for a conference. From that conference a plan emerged which might succeed in freeing the tanker if the norther held off for another day.

The officers and part of the crew returned to their stricken vessel at the crack of dawn. Then, it was found that not all the boilers were flooded, making it possible to get up enough steam to man the pumps. As the cargo was jettisoned the tanker righted herself and floated free, but was still several shallow sand bars away from deep water. Anchors were laid seaward from bow and stern and a tight pull was kept on the howsers with the winches. Slowly, as the black oil from the jettisoned cargo spread quiet-water all around the hull, the tanker was pulled broadside toward the open sea. As the vessel rose in the water it was observed that the breach in the hull was not so big as to preclude keeping water out of the engine room by using all cargo and sump pumps. By mid-afternoon there was a decided feeling of hope among the onlookers and the *Winifred* officers and crew that the tanker might be successfully salvaged—if the norther did not break before dark.

Fortunately, the norther delayed its fury until after the *Winifred* was towed inside the protected waters of the Panuco River. A few days later, salvage tugs arrived from Port Arthur to tow the tanker to a Texas drydock for repairs. In a month or so the *Winifred* was back in service carrying Mexican oil to the world markets.

What, if anything, is unusual about this incident? In order that you may understand, let me point out that the United States in early 1917 was not yet at war with Germany, hence, the officers of the *Tacoma* had no real authority over the American tank ship *Winifred* or its crew. Furthermore, the local general agent of the Mexican Gulf Oil Co. had no authority with respect to Gulf Refining Company's Marine Department vessels or personnel. However, everyone concerned cooperated and as a result, a tanker was saved to help fuel World War I.

Conditions in and around Tampico in those days bred that kind of wholehearted cooperation. We were united through adversity.

14

Riding the Rails During
the Mexican Revolution

For fifteen years or so after Porfirio Diaz relinquished
the Presidency, the national railways in Mexico had a
difficult time. Except in a few of the larger cities, paved highways were virtually non-existent. All heavy goods and people
traveling for any distance or in a hurry were moved by rail.
When the revolution broke out the railroads were the main
arteries for transporting troops and such artillery as was
available. Any large movement of troops of either side included a host of camp followers riding in, on top of, and
underneath, rail cars.

For the most part, the steam locomotives were fueled by
oil. All this oil originated either in Texas, or around Tampico
(Tuxpam had no rail connections) or came from the Isthmus de Tehuantepec. Consequently, oil trains moved everywhere across Mexico, for without fuel oil, all train service
came to a halt. This fact played a major part in the revolu-

tionary campaign. The tactics of Rebels was to interfere with any and all rail movement by blowing up tracks, wrecking trains, and destroying the fuel tank cars.

No longer could freight and passenger service be continued on schedule. Rolling stock was depleted and only on the main lines into Mexico City was the passenger train equipment first class. On the branch lines, what now were first class passenger coaches had been second or even third class in the pre-revolutionary days.

Rail travel during the revolution was hectic. Trains never left or arrived on time. Sometimes a train never reached its destination. At other times, it would arrive, but with only bits and pieces of the original train. However, a person could travel only by rail from Tampico to Mexico City or to Monterrey or to San Luis Potosi—there were no auto roads then

connecting these cities. There was no aeroplane service anywhere in Mexico.

Shooting up a passing train with rifle fire from ambush was
good sport and a daily occurrence. Dynamiting the tracks
was also frequent. Occasionally, the more hardy souls would
tear up the tracks and remove the rails to some inaccessible
place. But the worst damage was done in the mountainous
sections with "wild" engines or cars let loose down grade
against a passenger or freight train slowly steaming up grade.

I had to go from Tampico to Mexico City on business in
1917 (I believe it was). Since there were no convenient boats
scheduled via Veracruz, I decided to go by rail by way of
San Luis Potosi. The passenger train, with its usual armed
guard of soldiers on freight cars behind the engine and at
the end of the coaches, left Tampico only a few hours late.
Actually it was yesterday's train leaving today. I found a seat
in one of the "first class" coaches near the tail end of the
train, for I wanted to be where I could jump off most easily
if our train was attacked by Rebels. I had with me a minimum
of baggage but a lot of food. There were no restaurant cars
on the train and wayside eating places were catch-as-catch-
can at best. Westward ho, we steamed through Mendez,
Ebano, Coco, Las Palmas and on to Valles. At the latter station our train remained for hours for no evident reason.
Finally, I was told by the conductor that there were rumors
of a contemplated Rebel attack up ahead, probably in the
Tamasopa gorge, through which the railway ran from Micos

to Crucitos. We were waiting for orders to proceed. Micos lay at the eastern entrance to the narrow, twisting limestone gorge. Crucitos is located on the plateau (elevation 4,000 feet) at the west end of the gorge. The scenery from the valley to the table land ranks with the finest on the continent.

The railroad between Micos and Crucitos was single track, running for the most part on a shelf blown and hewn out of the almost vertical canyon walls. Should a wild train careen down this gorge and head-on into an upbound train the wreck would be terrible.

At last the orders came to proceed. Slowly our train got under way. I don't believe the crew or the soldiers were very happy to go on for fear of a catastrophy. I know the passengers were not, for many women were silently crying and a few folks were praying in the cluttered aisles. On we went without incident until we arrived at Micos. There again we stopped for another hour or so while the train men tried to telegraph Crucitos. Whether they got through, I don't know, however, we finally got the "All aboard" about dusk. If all went well we would be through the gorge and on top of the plateau by nightfall.

We went slowly up the steep grade. Soldiers were hanging out the doors of their cars and had festooned themselves on top of the coaches and all over the engine—they even were hanging onto the cow catcher. As we crept up and onward, I stationed myself on the platform of the rear coach, all set to jump should we hear the sound of an oncoming engine.

But for the tension, it would have been a grand sight— climbing up that canyon-like gorge with its subtropic vegetation down near the rushing waters. Unfortunately, the scene was marred by literally hundreds of wrecked railroad cars which had hurtled off the rails and down into the gorge. They lay twisted, upended and scrambled all over the steep canyon sides—a reminder of what would happen to our train if we met a wild one.

Finally, we got through to Crucitos all right. There, we learned that the Rebels had been repulsed in their attempt to steal a train but not before they had cut the telegraph. Had Crucitos been able to advise Micos that the way was clear all the passengers, crews and soldiers of our train would have been spared many anxious moments.

Early the next morning our train arrived at San Luis where the Mexico City bound passenger changed to the train from Monterrey and Laredo. The train for Mexico City left during the afternoon. It really appeared like a luxury train after the one we had traveled in from Tampico. I even had a berth in the Pullman. Before departure we were told there had been a skirmish between the Federals and Rebels just outside the city that morning. The Federals won. As our train moved southward the evidence of battle was visible from our windows. I counted twelve Rebel bodies dangling by the neck from the yardarm of as many telegraph poles—another grim reminder of the troublesome times.

Several years prior to the Tamasopa gorge trip, I had to go by rail from Tampico to Monterrey en route to the United States. The usual armed soldiers were along, riding the engine and a freight car up front. We departed about noon. Our train had moved along at a fair speed without incident for some 70 or 80 miles out of Tampico when it came to a jarring halt. In those revolutionary times, one's first impulse was to lie down on the floor below window level to avoid the ex-

pected fusilade of bullets. I went flat along with all the other passengers—all Mexicans except for one other American. When no shots were heard we got up and went out to reconnoiter. We found there had been no Rebel attack but that our locomotive had hit a cow and had been derailed by the impact.

As usual the telegraph line was out of commission. There was nothing that could be done until one of the crew had footed it ahead to the next section house where it was hoped to find a section gang to put our engine back on the rails. Hours went by as we waited. It grew dark and still no section hands.

By this time everyone was mighty hungry. The passengers milled around outside the cars. We were far from any signs of habitation. Bonfires were lit. Finally, some enterprising fellows went over to the dead cow and found she had been in prime condition and was not too badly mangled. One chap pulled out his knife and skinned the cow sufficiently to carve off several pieces of the loin. Soon we were all having a jolly barbecue over the open fires to the music of guitars which some of the passengers had with them. It was an excellent feast.

At long last the section hands arrived by hand car and in a matter of another hour our engine was back on the track none the worse for the accident.

Shortly before dawn, not far from Monterrey, our train was halted again. We had been flagged to a stop by a section crew. A bridge had been blown up by the Rebels the day before, around which a shoo fly had been laid off the road bed, down across the dry stream bed and up the opposite bank to the main right of way. Our train would have to take this shoo fly fast in order to make the grade on the opposite side. Now I was dozing and didn't bother to get up and out with the other passengers. I felt our train back up for a half mile or so and then gather speed again in the foward direction. It must have hit the shoo fly going at least 20 miles an hour. As our train bowled off the right of way and down the ravine over the temporary track, I thought we were going into the ditch and came to my feet in a hurry. I was sure scared. But needlessly, for the train made it to the other side and back onto the main line without jumping the track. Was my face red, when we were safely on our way.

In ordinary times the rail trip from Veracruz to Mexico City is most enjoyable and scenic. In 424 kilometers (roughly 265 miles) as the train goes, one rises from sea level to an elevation of over 7,400 feet. Actually, the high point in the journey is at Boca del Monte (K 173) 7844 feet above Veracruz. From Paso del Macho (K 76) to Cordoba (K 106) the elevation rises 1,200 feet. From Nogales (K 140), a little over 5 miles west of Orizaba, to Maltrata (K 152) the train climbs over 1,500 feet.

Between Paso del Macho and Maltrata is some of the most scenic country in America. From the damp tropics to the semi-arid plateau country of the temperate zone in a matter of a few hours — almost continuously in sight of snow-capped Mount Orizaba, which rises 18,225 feet above the sea.

Because, nowadays, the tourist in Mexico usually travels by plane or auto, few recent visitors have sensed the scenic pleasure and thrills of a train journey from Veracruz to Mexico City via Cordoba and Orizaba. For the benefit of those recent visitors, I am including herein liberal passages from *Terry's Guide to Mexico*—the 1923 Revised Edition.*

76 K. Paso del Macho (Mule Pass) 1,500 feet. The warm, humid air of the coast lands, laden with the pungent smell of rank, tropical vegetation, merges into waves of cooler mountain air in which the senses register faint piny odors. The myriad birds that impart life and color to the lagoons adjacent to Veracruz rarely pass the dividing line between the foothills and the mountains, as the keen-eyed eagles are sharp-taloned hawks which infest the higher reaches and not to the liking of timid egrets, ducks, parakeets and similar species.

97 K. Paraje Nuevo. The ascent becomes visibly steeper and sharp 4% grades make the powerful engines snort and wheeze till the surrounding hills fling back the echo of their efforts. . . .

_____

*Published by Houghton Mifflin Company, Boston and New York.

Soon the rank vegetation of the tropics, and the giant hot country trees garlanded with beautifully tinted orchids drop silently behind, like fogged runners in an unequal race. Luxuriant bananas flank the railway and beneath their graceful fronds appear the red berries of ripening coffee. Through gaps in the hills one gets fine vistas of extensive cane fields. The mountains up which we are now climbing show belting forests of pine on their verdant sides. The scenery is charming. The languor induced by the humidity of the coastal region has vanished at the touch, and the tonic effect, of the bracing air of the highlands.

And so on to Cordoba (K 106).

114 K. Fortin, so-called because of a little fortress near by ... the scenery becomes grandly beautiful, and we soon reach one of the most weird and fearsome passes on the line. The train moves slowly, turns sharply to the right and cautiously glides down one side of the deep Metlac Barranca. On the other side of a yawning ravine, in the depths of which a tropical river churns its way, is another line of rails, on a terrace cut from the side of a precipice at an angle similar to that of a toboggan slide. Five tunnels interrupt this line before it reaches the higher level and turns the flank of the hill. The train glides very slowly and gingerly across the Metlac bridge, a very skillful piece of engineering work 350 ft. long, built on a curve of 325 ft. radius, on a 3% grade, 92 ft. above the river.... When a long train is winding across it, the horseshoe effect is very striking. . . . As the train creeps up the flank of the opposite mountain the Barranca widens and exposes tropical charms to the delighted eye. Magnificent forest trees, covered with yellow, purple and

pink blossoms, palms of many kinds and patches of luxuriant jungle, bright with scores of different brilliant flowers or creepers which throw themselves from one tree top to another as they tower above the tangled undergrowth, are seen, while anon a glimpse of a fair valley is had: a vale snuggled between sheltering hills, bathed in sunshine and rank with vegetation of the lower tropics. Dainty little waterfalls are revealed up the glens as the train climbs by, while others rush under the culverts to leap into mid-air and lose themselves in clouds of mist and spray, shot with all the colors of the rainbow. . . . They (tunnels) are so numerous that at times the locomotive will be in one and the last car of the train in another. . . . The magnificent cone of Orizaba is again visible, a white and serene apothesis against the bosom of the blue sky.

122 K. Sumidero, in the heart of the Coffee Zone, which extends from Paso del Macho to Orizaba.

134 K. Orizaba (4,028 ft) a quaint and unusually attractive provincial city . . . picturesquely situated in a green, well-watered valley where eternal springtime reigns, midway between the tropics and the cool table land of the higher reaches. It occupies the site of an Indian village which is said to have existed centuries before the Spaniards came . . . the Orizaba (river), plunges through a rocky ravine in the city, and adds a picturesque charm to it.

140 K. Nogales. The train enters a gloomy barranca, El Infiernillo—little hell—and crosses dizzy acclivities, passing thru tunnels and over streams which have worn deep chasms in the trap-rock . . . we pass a number of pretty waterfalls and cascades . . . the scenery changes. Conifers and mountain scruboaks take the place of banana and coffee groves.

152 K. Maltrata (5544 ft). The vale is encircled by tall hills, rising grandly, above which is the splendid cone of Orizaba. Peach trees are plentiful and the train is met at the station by a score or more of Indian women with peaches, pomegranates, avocado-pears, tamales, tortillas and confits for sale. . . . A beautiful waterfall plunges into a gorge on the left. The train

zig-zags up the hills, approaching them over great curves and winning them by daring runs across terraces cut from their sides. In retrospect we can trace the road below as it doubles and twists and loops its way downward among the valleys; at times as many as six lines of rails are visible, like silver ribbons in the depths, with many aerial, spider-like bridges, which from here seem to dip like steel flumes.... The air grows perceptibly cooler.

166 K. Alta Luz. . . . We have reached a gradient of nearly 5% through rock-cuts hung with ferns, dripping with water and redolent with wild flowers. . . . The environing hills are clothed in pine and oaks and giant cacti cling like huge green rosettes to the mountain wall. The scene is more like New Hampshire than tropical Mexico. Here the train (which on rainy days often passes through low-lying clouds) stands 2,919 ft. higher than the top most point of Mt. Washington and the panorama is magnificient. . . . Winners bridge (90 ft. long) spans a yawning chasm from the ridge of which the scenery is awe-inspiring and of surpassing grandeur.

173 K. Boca del Monte . . . 7,849 ft. above Veracruz and the sea. Since leaving that part we have climbed 1½ miles above the fortress of San Juan de Ulua and we have touched three zones—the tierra caliente, tierra templada and tierra fria.

I know of no better description of that scenic journey from the sea to the plateau in Central Mexico than the foregoing from Terry's Guide. I have personally made that rail trip a number of times in years past and hope to do it again one day soon. It is not the same by highway I know, because I drove to Cordoba and Fortin by car from Mexico City only a few years ago.

15

Fires and Tanks

During my residence in Tampico a number of fires occurred in and around the city. None was catastrophic, though several resulted in serious loss to property. Three of these fires stand out in my memory, more because of their comic aspects than their seriousness.

In those days the Tampico fire brigade was not mechanized. Hose carts and hand pumps mounted on four wheels (operated by handles, up and down, like a railroad hand car) were pulled to the fire by man power or tied onto a Ford car if one happened along and could be pressed into service. Ladders and axes were carried on the shoulders of the firemen.

The firemen had wonderful uniforms, more colorful than practical. Heavy white rubber helmets, blue wool coats with large brass buttons, brilliant red pants and sometimes white rubber boots which were kept spanking clean. Whenever the fire alarm sounded the several firemen scurried home to don their uniforms before they would report for duty. The delay for getting properly dressed was of no great moment to either the firemen or the public—notwithstanding someone's property was burning.

The fire alarm system was rather unique. When a fire occurred a bugler sounded off at the fire station. Then he hurried to another street corner, nearer the blaze and sounded off again to the four corners of the compass. And so on, until he arrived at the fire, where he would stand on the nearest street corner and continue to blow his trusty bugle until the firemen arrived on the scene.

The sight and sound of the bugle, the rush of fancy dressed firemen hauling their dinky apparatus, the inpouring of armed police, the swarms of onlookers and looters shouting advice to anybody and everybody, and the consequent snarl in mule drawn train cars and other wheeled traffic created a comic relief of bedlam.

On one occasion, Tampico's only American grocery store caught fire. As soon as the firemen were on the scene volunteers were called for to carry stock out onto the sidewalk. The many volunteers soon removed much of the stock from the building, although most of the groceries and canned goods kept right on moving away from the fire, to the homes of the volunteers. For days those "volunteer" firemen enjoyed American food, tinned and otherwise, such as they had never tasted before. Needless to say that grocery store stock was practically a total loss to the owner.

Another time, fire broke out during the night in a small *tienda* across the street from the office of the Mexican Gulf Oil Company. By the time I reached the scene the fire had made such headway that it looked, for a while, as though our building and others nearby would also be involved. Our office building was owned by Dr. Autrey (a man of German descent), druggist by trade, who had made a small fortune out of a calentura remedy. His drugstore was on the first floor, while our offices were located on the three floors above.

Behind the *tienda* several steel drums of gasoline and kerosene were stored. These had been rolled out and up-ended in the street, with soldiers standing by to prevent looting. The blaze spread and got out of control. The scene of the fire was several city blocks from the river—too far away for the hand pumps to send any considerable stream of water. Actually the water playing on the fire resembled tired cooked macaroni and was about as effective.

The *tienda* was a total loss.

When the fire spread and threatened to involve an adjacent multiple-storied bottling works the valiant firemen broke into that building and started to wreck and dismantle the machinery, much to the anguish of its owner.

As the fire moved away from our building, Dr. Autrey and our company personnel breathed easier. However, we were shocked into action when we saw that a vigilant policeman had placed his lighted kerosene lantern down on top of one of the drums of gasoline—wet with fluid which had splashed out of the open bung hole. The lantern was quickly removed by Dr. Autrey, who, with an amazing breadth of Spanish invective, told off the policeman, his employers, his family and his ancestors. Speechless, the policeman salvaged his lantern and slunk off to a less vulnerable vantage point. Only then did we really relax.

The most spectacular fire that I witnessed in Tampico occurred in the Custom House yard. It was a comic opera affair. This is what happened.

Mexico has no good coal deposits, only brown coal or lignite from the region around Monterrey. Some of the Spanish steamship lines made it known to the authorities that their steamers would not call at Tampico unless coal bunkers were available there, so an agreement was made to supply these Spanish vessels with brown coal. Over a period of months train load after train load of lignite was brought to Tampico and dumped in a huge pile along the tracks back of the Custom House. Evidently the coal did not meet steaming requirements, and it stood there, black and bleak, for several years.

One day the pile was noticed to be smoking near the top. The alarm was sounded, bugles blew, and in due course Tampico's fire brigade in full regalia and with all necessary equipment was on hand. The corps were lined up in their Sunday best uniforms, looking like little tin soldiers. Finally, ladders were laid prone on the slopes of the coal heap and up these scrambled the firemen dragging their little hoses from which emanated pitiful streams of water from the river. The water was about as effective as spitting into a bonfire. Axes and shovels were called into play. More hoses were laid and more firemen scrambled around the coal fire, shouting and struggling, as the bugler bugled. In a matter of minutes all the white helmets, red pants, blue coats, white boots, as well as the faces and hands of the firemen were sooty black. The brigade resembled black ants scampering up and down a huge smoking black ant hill. It really was a funny sight from the onlookers' point of view. There was no significant loss of property but the loss of firemen's dignity must have been considerable. A few days later a heavy downpour of rain quenched the fire and, after a lapse of some months, the brown coal was hauled away by train, whence it came.

Before the era of gas-tight steel storage for crude and refined petroleum, tank fires in Mexico were almost as common as thunderstorms. The oil produced in the Panuco-Topila area was heavy (11° to 12° gravity) and that produced in the South Country was only somewhat lighter (20° to 27° gravity), but the admixture of the sour gas made both crudes highly combustible.

During the days of the great oil boom in Mexico, from 1910-1922, the largest storage tanks held some 55,000 barrels and were constructed of riveted plates in the shell and bottom. The roofs were wooden, upheld by interior wooden supports, over which thin sheets of steel were tacked. When such tanks were being filled gas escaped around the rim of the roof as well as from the gas vent and the gauger's hatch in the roof.

The rising stream of escaping gas from oil tanks was a perfect lightning conductor. Seldom was there a severe electric storm in the oil fields or around the terminals where the oil tankships were loaded, that one or more crude storage tanks was not struck and burned. In the Tampico area, during one such storm, six tanks were blazing at one time, filling the heavy atmosphere with huge billowing clouds of black smoke. It made one think of Dante's inferno—the oily black pale hovering overhead into which flames burst, sometimes more than a thousand feet above the burning tanks.

I witnessed many such tank fires in Mexico, both in close proximity and from a distance. Chemical fire fighting equipment had not then been perfected. Water quenching is virtually impossible in the case of an unroofed tank in which up to 50,000 barrels of heavy oil is burning. Steam helps to control the blaze but is seldom completely effective unless it can blanket the blaze and snuff out the fire. Under the circumstances, when an oil tank caught fire (usually the roof was blown off by the explosion), the operator bled off as much oil as possible through the bottom connections on the tank before the inevitable "boil."

The boil occurs when the blaze heats up the mixture of sediment, oil and water in the tank bottoms to such a temperature that the tank literally boils over. It is not a slow boil, but rather resembles an explosion in that practically all the remaining contents is hurled hundreds of feet into the air where much of the fluid is burned. The boil is extremely dangerous for any living animal or person close to the tank, because no one can predict with certainty when or where the burning liquid will fall. I've seen men burned to a crisp in the falling inferno hundreds of feet away from the burning tank, trapped by a fence or other obstacle in their run for life. The roar and heat

of the fire, the billowing black smoke and the uncertainty of where and when the tank will boil made the oil tank fires in Mexico an awful experience—now a vivid haunting memory.

The company I was connected with in Mexico had its tanker loading terminal on the Panuco River some five miles above the city of Tampico. One day, while loading a tanker, the loading tank was struck by lightning and fired. The tank was almost full at the time. Since the operators knew a boil was unlikely until the tank's contents had been nearly all consumed they kept the pumps busy, moving oil from the bottom connections of the burning tank to the tanker. The shell plates got so hot one could see the silhouette of the unburned fluid through the sides of the tank. This was our visual gauge. We had another check too—temperature of the fluid as it passed through the pumps. Lower and lower went the silhouette and hotter and hotter became the crude passing to the tanker. Everyone feared that the tank might boil over on the camp and tanker or that the hot oil might create an explosive condition in the tanker. Finally, it was decided to cease the transfer when the fluid reached a temperature of 175° Fahrenheit. When the pumps were stopped, the fluid level in the burning tank was barely five or six feet above tank bottom. Promptly the tanker cast off her lines and anchored in mid stream, while the camp operators ordered everyone on shore to a safe distance from the blazing tank. Within the half hour the tank boiled, but the contents were so low that no material damage was done to the plant by the fall out and no one was injured.

Nowadays, with all welded, all steel gas-tight tankage for both crude and refined products, oil fires occasioned by lightning are almost unheard of. Usually the exception can be traced to a gas leak in the upper portion of the tank.

In the old days earthen fire walls were built around each tank or maybe a battery of tanks. The walls were constructed to be able to catch and hold at least two-thirds the capacity of tank or tanks encircled, should the tank split for any reason, or should the contents catch fire, and a boil result. Today, fire walls are no longer really necessary but this precautionary measure is still followed by most companies.

Mexican Gulf Oil Company's original tank farm layout near Tampico was located in a semi-swamp area only a few feet above Panuco River level. The storage tanks had not been erected on piles and so, in a few years, began to sink from sheer weight of contents. Even the pump station was located on such low ground that it had to be surrounded by an earthen dike to keep out surface water. There was no higher ground nearby, but something had to be done.

Our company had engaged a dredge to deepen the channel in the Panuco in front of our terminal dock so that tank vessels could be loaded to the maximum depth permitted over the outer bar of the river. The spoil from this dredging operation would be piped back into the tank farm and allowed to settle all around the tanks and pump station. Huge retaining dikes were built at the back and sides of the tank farm to hold the spoil. The level of the dredged material, when in place and settled, would be several feet above the dock level.

When all was ready, the dredging began and in a matter of weeks the tank farm was flooded with spoil. When the job was finished one could hardly see the pump station, nestled down inside of its dike, and some of the tanks were buried in the spoil up to their middle.

These tanks, like most others in the Tampico area, had wooden roofs overlaid with sheet iron. The problem was how to raise and move these tanks intact. Norman Perry was then our pipeline and terminal superintendent (later he was transferred to Houston and became a vice president of the Gulf Pipe Line Company). Norman was a practical fellow who got the impossible done, soonest. He devised a scheme and it worked.

Soon as the spoil was dry and firm, new grades were built for each tank on the higher level some feet away from the old sites. Then a small low dike was built, enveloping the old and new grades. That done, the tank to be moved was pumped dry and a ditch was dug all around the shell to below the bottom plates. Steel cables were strung around the shell and up and over the roof to "tie" it down securely to the shell. When all was ready, water was pumped into the ditch until the empty tank bobbed up like a cork. The pumping continued until the water level inside the retaining wall was over the level of the new tank grade. Then by man power alone the empty tank was floated over to its new grade. The water inside the retaining wall was then pumped out and the tank settled into position, level and intact except for minor damage to some of the wooden roof members. This operation was successfully repeated until all tanks were on high ground. Not a single tank had to be rebuilt. One tank was even floated onto such a high grade that it could be used to gravity load our tankers at the terminal dock.

16

Taming Wild Wells

During the past 100 years, since the completion of
the famous Colonel E. L. Drake oil well in Pennsylvania, there have been many hundreds of wells in this
country and abroad which have come in out of control—
"wild," as expressed in the industry. Some of these wild ones
caught fire and burned until all the oil and gas from the
underground had been exhausted, leaving a crater from
which salt water still exudes. However, for the most part
these wild ones were eventually tamed (capped or cemented
off) whether they caught fire or not.

Fighting a wild oil or gas well, especially if it is burning,
is a very hazardous business. In the early days the work of
taming was done by volunteer well men but in recent years
the fighting has been done mostly by professional experts, of
which Myron Kinley and Red Adair are among the best
known.

If an oil or gas well gets out of control, every effort is made
to keep the flow from catching fire. No naked lights are permitted around the wild well and water and steam lines are

rigged so as to snuff the blaze in case the flow does ignite. Should the flow catch fire, it is then necessary to cool the well connection with steam and water (in order to prevent the control connections from being burned off) while making ready to attempt to close the master gate. Nowadays, in case of a bad fire enveloping the well connection, it is common practice for the fighters to dynamite the upper connections in order to cause the flow and fire to go straight up. When the flow and fire are going straight up in the air, under favorable wind conditions, well men can get at the connections below the fire and either repair or replace them to permit the well's being closed in.

Many fighters have been seriously injured, badly burned or even killed in trying to control wild oil and gas wells. It is extremely dangerous work. Notwithstanding, a wild oil or gas well is an awe inspiring sight, more especially if it is a big gusher afire.

In the era 1904-1922, Mexico had many gushers. Except for San Diego No. 3 (Dos Bocas), all the wild ones were eventually brought under control. In 1922 salt water encroachment in the underground oil reservoir rock brought an end to the gusher completions in the well-known Golden Lane.

In these days of improved drilling techniques it seems strange that 50 years ago wells were allowed to get out of control in Mexico, rather deliberately. There, it was then the practice to drill the upper hole with rotary tools down to the pay limestone and to complete the hole with cable tools. The oil men of my day in Mexico held that if a well did not come in with enough "push" to blow the drilling tools out of the hole it really was not much of a well—hardly worth bothering about.

Every wild oil well is a problem to control. Each fight is packed with more or less human interest, as well as exciting exploits.

Mexico had scores of wild wells—too many to all be mentioned herein. However, there follows a few typical incidents in which I was involved to some extent.

The Chinampa No. 1 (Lot 95 Chinampa) well was completed in August 1919 at a depth of 2,130 feet. It was brought in under control and was never literally wild. However, a leak in the surface connections at the well head produced an amusing incident that can now be told.

The location was in a small valley. The derrick was not elevated on stilts, so, in order to get the master gate and drilling nipple below the wooden derrick floor, a deep cellar was dug. After the well was completed and connected to the pipeline, a serious leak developed and flooded the cellar. For some reason it was not thought feasible either to pump out or to drain the cellar in order to get at the loose connections. The well men were certain of the cause of the trouble, and felt that the leak could be controlled if they could get at the connections.

A deep sea diver from Tuxpam was sent for. In due course he arrived at the site and was instructed as to just what he should do beneath the surface of the oil in the cellar. When he fully understood what to do and where to do it, his heavy rubber suit was donned, his helmet screwed on and his air pumps started. Wrench in hand, he lumbered over to the ladder which had been lowered into the inky black, sulphurous smelling oil. Down he clambered until his head completely disappeared below the oil surface. We waited breathlessly for about a minute, when up popped his oil besmirched helmet. He came up the ladder and out of the cellar much faster than he went in. Soon as the diver got out he waved his arms frantically and motioned for his helmet to be removed first. It took only a few moments to loosen the helmet bolts and remove it from the rest of his suit. A cloud of hot vapor issued from inside the diver's gear—his face was red as a beet and tears flowed from his eyes.

We were stunned. But then, when we saw that he was really none the worse for the experience, it dawned on us what had happened and all of us—except the diver—burst out laughing. Someone had bungled. In our anxiety to get the job done we had completely forgotten to tell the diver that the fluid in the cellar was hot. The oil in that well reached the surface with a temperature in excess of 150° Fahrenheit —too hot for comfortable immersion, especially when clad in a heavy sealed rubber diving suit.

To no avail we tried to persuade the diver to have another go at it. Nothing doing. He just walked off the job, more angry than parboiled.

When that happened one of the well men volunteered to do the job without benefit of either diving suit or clothes of any kind. So, with ears packed with cotton and compression grease, naked as a jay bird, wrench tied around his waist, the volunteer quickly descended the ladder. Within a minute he was out again looking like a black oily scarecrow. Soon as he had wiped the oil from his face, nose, eyes and ears he said that his job was successful—the leak had been stopped. Our "hero" suffered no burns of consequence or any other ill effects from his hot oil bath.

Mexican Gulf Oil Company drilled four wells on Lot 190 Amatlan in 1921 and 1922. Together these wells produced over seven million barrels of oil in less than two years before salt water encroachment caused the production to be "pinched back."

Amatlan No. 14, the discovery well, blew in a huge gasser on April 26, 1921 at a depth of 1,970 feet. The tools were blown out of the hole and knocked off the crown block at the top of the wooden derrick but without igniting the flow. The roar of the tremendous column of gas—misty white, like steam—was deafening. The concussion shook the rig and the ground around. (The air vibration was so great that all my close-up camera shots came out blurred.) Even before there was any sign of oil in the flow, the force of the gas and its vibration had blown the derrick down to the first girt. After a few hours black oil began to show in the flow and soon it was all black. Its highest plume was calculated to be over 700 feet above the ground when photographed, shortly after the master gate was partially closed.

It was not considered safe to close in the well entirely because the tremendous flow pressure quite obviously exceeded the test strength of the master gate. So the well was allowed to flow wild while the crews stabbed a heavier-test valve over the master gate and strengthened all the connections by additional clamps and rods to tie the new valve securely to the surface casing below. In order to do this the first girt of the derrick was partially rebuilt and reinforced to carry the block and tackle with which the heavy new gate would be swung over the flow and down onto the well connections.

In those days the iron master gates used in Mexico were made by Darling and the one chosen for Amatlan No. 14 weighed around two tons. In spite of that great weight the drilling crew had trouble with stabbing the open valve over the flow and onto the connections. The oil gushed out with such force that on the first attempt the heavy valve bobbed around in and out of the flow like a cork in a fountain.

The poisonous gas was so bad and knocked men out so quickly that each man on the derrick floor had a rope around his waist so that, if he collapsed, one of his colleagues on the ground could pull him out of danger. We did not have adequate gas masks in Mexico in those days. The vibration and roar were so great that all men on the derrick had their ears packed with cotton and compression grease over which a felt hat was tied down tight. All orders, close in around the well, were conveyed by pantomime from one man to another. The well was finally capped after several days, without fire, loss of life or serious injury to any of the well crew. But it was a nasty job.

Thus another wild Mexican gusher was tamed.

The Mexican Gulf Oil Company drilled a total of eleven wells on its 330 acres of checkerboard leases chosen from International Petroleum Company's Toteco property consisting of over 7,500 acres. Those eleven wells produced over 40 million barrels of crude petroleum in a few years. The largest producer of these eleven wells was No. 4, which blew in wild and caught fire on September 14, 1921 from a depth of 1,907 feet.

Toteco No. 4 site was on a hillside in a large clearing in the woods. The oil companies in Mexico had by this time learned their lesson about the hazards of cellars and so the derrick floor for this well was elevated high above the ground, with all connections exposed. Because so many previous wells' connections had suffered damage from falling drilling tools when the wild ones blew in, on Toteco No. 4 the derrick floor was covered with iron tank plate all around the drilling nipple. As a further precaution a long rod extension had been fixed to the stem of the master gate valve, on the outer end of which was a large wheel to make for easy turning in any emergency. Otherwise the well was rigged similar to other wells in the area, including the wooden derrick (steel derricks were not yet in vogue). In those days all drilling in Mexico was done with steam rigs.

The story of the seven day battle to control Toteco No. 4, appeared in the Houston, Texas, *Chronicle* on September 26, 1921:

GRAPHIC STORY OF FIGHTING
MEXICAN OIL GUSHER FIRE
READS LIKE TRENCH BATTLE

Tampico, Mexico, Sept. 22—(By Mail.)—The graphic story of how, what the world calls heroism but which is better known here in the oil fields as just plain guts, conquered one of the greatest fires in the history of the oil industry and saved what may prove to be the greatest of all the great Mexican oil wells from destruction, was told today by Charles W. Hamilton, General Agent of the Mexican Gulf Oil Company, just back from Toteco, where he directed the combined efforts of crews from six great oil companies in the successful fight against the fire which broke out in Toteco No. 4, a well with a capacity of considerably more than 100,000 barrels a day, brought in September 14. The tremendous force of the well when it was brought in hurled the tools against the crown block, and sparks from the contact instantly changed the great gusher of black gold to a roaring tower of flame more than 1,000 feet high.

Burned Shoes Off Feet.

"I don't take a bit of credit for this to myself," Mr. Hamilton said. "I feel that the credit is due to the courage, fidelity, resourcefulness, and, above all, co-operation of all the men engaged. It was one man, a Greek named Charley Chuck, employed by the International Company, who climbed upon the tank sheet, using the bolts for steps, and finally put a Stilson wrench on the valve stem which enabled us to close the gate. But it was the courage and co-operation of more than 100 men, just as ready as he and just as capable in the parts of the job which fell to them, which made his achievement possible. Every man did his duty, whether it was fighting the fire in heat so intense that it continually burned the shoes off the feet of the fire fighters or installing boilers and laying water lines, without the aid of which no one could have approached the fire.

"The fire would have been put out in 18 hours but for the lack of water. The first night of the fire a crew of Mexican Gulf boys fought their way up to it, but falling timbers when the fire began had bent the tank sheet in such a way that it was impossible to shut off the valve. It was necessary to take off the extension and splice on another extension.

"The pressure of the well was so great that the flames shot more than 1,000 feet into the air when it was wide open. Even when it was pinched in to about 15,000 barrels the flames rose more than 300 feet, engineers estimated."

Trench Warfare.

"Our plan of campaign was to fight the fire from behind three trenches, or corrugated iron shields. From the trench farthest from the fire men played water on those in the trench ahead, and they in turn on the men in the first. From the first, men wearing ponchos made of blankets and cowled like monks in wet blankets, rushed on up to the tower of flame. Steady streams of water were to be played on these men to prevent their clothing from igniting in the terrible heat and incinerating them, and they also dragged hose. Eighteen boilers were installed to supply steam and cool water for the hose, but time after time, too, sheets of burning tar, caused by sudden veerings of the wind, fell between the men at the well and safety but every time, with a spirit of the noblest cause, they kept their heads and played their hose on each other, saving each other from fearful death.

"The second day of the fire we managed to close the gate valve all but two turns, pinching in the flow from more than 100,000 barrels to about 15,000 barrels, but then oil and gas began to leak around the valve stem. The ground was burned for a radius of more than 500 feet, and we had to keep a large supply of shoes on hand as the men's shoes constantly were catching fire from the heat of the ground.

"After the second day we called on other companies for help and the Aguila, Huasteca, Transcontinental, Metropolitan and International companies at once responded and co-operated with us to the limit of their powers. An advisory committee of five was appointed to counsel with me in the campaign, consisting of Mr. Craig of the Aguila company, Chairman; Mr. Flick of the Huasteca, Mr. Chaney of the International, Mr. Arner of the Transcontinental and Mr. Gilliam, a contractor. Drilling Superintendent Hay of the Mexican Gulf was my assistant and in direct charge of the fire fighting forces."

Question of Water.

"From the beginning it was only a question of getting enough water. Several sources of supply on which we counted proved inadequate. In one case we counted on a well which had been closed in because of salt water in the Amatlan field to supply us both volume and pressure, but when we laid water lines to it and uncapped it, it began flowing pure oil instead, at the rate of about 400 barrels a day. Everyone knew that as soon as we got enough water for steam and to play on the men going into the fire that the ground fires and the fire on the connections could be extinguished and the rest would be comparatively easy. But everyone also knew that the pressure we had was likely to give out at any moment, and the nerve of the men who plunged in time after time can be better appreciated when that is remembered."

Fighter Crazed by Heat.

"Some idea of the strain under which the men worked can be gained by the fact that after three days of it one of our men, Herbert Grace of Denver, became temporarily deranged, took a gun from a Mexican guard and began to shoot up the camp. While trying to disarm him, another Mexican soldier fired, the bullet striking Carl R. Tabb of Lufkin, Texas, killing him instantly. Grace then was wounded and disarmed.

"But after many trials the psychological moment came. The ground fires and the fire in the cellar were out, the pressure in the water lines was abundant, and the men then on duty in the front trench considered themselves lucky. Everything worked perfectly as the men selected for the final dash went in. Steady streams of water poured on them from the nozzles and all the ground around them was soaked.

"When Charley Chuck, a Greek, working for the International Company, reached the tank sheet which had been such a serious obstacle to fighting the fire, he climbed up on it, using the bolts for a ladder, and put a Stilson wrench on the valve stem. To that he attached wire and then, from a safe distance, the gate valve was closed by pulling on the wire, and the great fire which a moment before had made the night as bright as day blinked out as if an electric switch had been turned.

"The great well apparently was not damaged at all. We believe it is going to be one of the greatest producers in Mexico. It is shallower than any other well in Mexico, being only 1,324 feet below sea level."

The newspaper credits Charley with being a Greek but actually, to the best of my recollection, he was a Chek. Whatever nationality, Charley was a brave man.

However, in order to put the record straight, I must say now that Charley's exploit was not part of the approved plan. It really was not necessary to take such a risk. What he did, he did on his own in the dead of night with half of his pipeline shift. I have reason to believe his unusual courage was sparked by tequila but, if so, that does not detract one whit from this incredible feat.

In the foregoing *Houston Chronicle* article about Toteco No. 4 mention is made of Herbert Grace who ran amuck during the fire. There are some features of this episode which bear disclosure, after all these years.

I had not personally known Grace before the Toteco fire, although he was one of Gulf's well men. When I first saw him in the Toteco Camp he was stark naked sitting on the grassy slope in front of the camp bunkhouses. I went over to him and asked the "why's and wherefor's." He said he had breathed fire while around the burning well and was burning up inside. He looked to me more drunk than sick, but I arranged to have him sent on up to Tepetate to Gulf's field hospital for observation. (Later, some of the boys told me that they had seen Grace drinking tequila when off duty.)

Some 36 hours after I first saw him—it was about 2 A.M. —I was walking away from the camp office down the board-

walk in front of the bunkhouses with our pipeline superintendent, Eddie Morend. All of a sudden out of the shadows
came Grace, running toward us—machete in one hand and
pistol in the other—yelling that the Germans were coming
and he was going to kill Epley (the lame telegraph operator)
who, he shouted, was a spy. We dared not stop him, armed
as he was armed. So we stepped off the sidewalk as he
darted on toward the camp office. When he had passed us
we shouted as loud as we could to Epley to watch out for
Grace. Then we circled back. By the time we reached the
shack and entered, Epley had grappled with Grace and had
taken the machete but not the pistol. Grace had Epley and
the other boys who were in the shack lined up facing the
menacing pistol in his hand.

Because of the fire, it was as light as a summer's eve under
a full moon. One could read a newspaper outside, although
it was way past midnight and the camp was fully a half mile
from the burning well. The inside of the office was bril-
liantly lighted with electric lights and the reflected glow of
the burning well. Two bedrooms flanked either side of the
center office room.

Grace recognized me soon as I stepped inside and spoke
politely to me. I remonstrated with him to put down his
pistol and go to bed but he refused. None of us were armed
and in any event we would have hesitated to shoot him in
cold blood, for up to now he had done nothing but threaten
us.

Finally I said, "Grace, I am going to my bedroom behind
you for much needed sleep and you had best go along off to
your own bunk." Grace made no move to stop me as I passed
him. The inside of this wing-bedroom was dark as pitch. Two
cots were there—mine and a cot for the visiting manager of
another company. Our visitor was ostensibly asleep under his
blankets but I sensed he was awake. I sat on my cot facing
Grace standing in the doorway with his back toward me. How

could I overwhelm him without getting shot, perhaps by mistake? Thus I pondered and sweated. At last I called out to Grace to come on in and sit down with me. He did, but kept his pistol cocked and leveled at my belly. Then he noticed a movement on the cot opposite and allowed aloud that there was one German he would kill. However, I talked him out of doing anything rash, explaining that the other fellow was a VIP visitor and not a spy.

I thought to myself, "I must get his gun." But as I tensed to grab his pistol arm he shoved the pistol into my ribs and said, "No you don't Mr. Hamilton." With that he got up and walked out into the office and lined up the fellows who had remained.

I got up and followed Grace, saying, "If you won't go to bed at least come on over to the mess house and get some food." Maybe hot food would counteract the tequila which by now I was sure he had had a "snort" of. Grace acquiesced and marshalled us all ahead of him at the point of his gun. In the mess hall he sat on one of the benches at the long table, between Epley and me; the others ranged around. He still had his pistol drawn. We ordered eggs, bacon and coffee from the Chinaman who ran the mess 24 hours a day during the fire. A young Chinese boy came in to wait on the table. Grace didn't like his looks so ordered him at pistol point to get out. The poor lad was so scared that he dove into a pile of potato sacks in the corner of the room and buried himself out of sight. Grace dallied with the food, one handed, but did not really eat. Epley was watching closely. I saw his hand reach out for the catsup bottle and I sensed he was going to try to bean Grace, but Grace was too smart for him. He said, "Ep, what are you going to do with that bottle?" Epley said, rather quavering, "Why, I like catsup in my coffee" and proceeded to fill his cup half full and down it all in one gulp.

When we saw we were not getting anywhere with Grace and food, we talked him into going outside. I again importuned him to go to his bunkhouse and to bed. At last he agreed and went off down the walk. We saw him turn off the main walk toward his house and mount the steps. Unfortunately, he spotted a sleeping Mexican soldier at one end of the porch. He looked down at the sarape covered form, hesitated, then in one motion he kicked the soldier off the porch, grabbed the soldier's rifle and jumped off the porch. Grace ran down the hill a few steps, then knelt and raised the rifle. Two shots rang out on the night air as he ran into the shadows between the camp and the burning well.

Morend and I ran toward the bunkhouse where we found one of our boiler firemen had been killed by Grace's shots. One bullet had penetrated the wooden wall of the bunkhouse and passed through the head of Carl Tabb who was sleeping at the time. I ran on down to the warehouse where we had a telephone and alerted the well crew, saying, "Grace is loco and armed and was last seen going up the hill toward the well." Also I called the officer of the guard and told him that if he saw Grace to "Shoot to kill if necessary. He's crazy, he has killed a man and is still armed with both a rifle and a pistol." We dared not go after him, in the shadows of the woods, for we were all unarmed except the soldiers. I waited at the telephone, hoping against hope no one else would get hurt.

Minutes passed and still no word came from the well that Grace had been seen. While we waited tensely, someone in the bunkhouse, where Tabb had been killed, hollered out, "Here he comes," and then jumped out of one of the screened windows, clad only in long white underwear, and dashed off into the shadows. My nerves broke and I, too, ran for the bushes along with another fellow. Each of us thought Grace was after us personally. Soon as we reached the brush we both looked about rather sheepishly and then returned to the warehouse. It was as much as thirty minutes—perhaps more —before my phone rang and a voice cryptically said, "We've got him," and hung up.

As near as I could ever ascertain, it seems that Grace burst out of the shadows on the hill into the full glare of the burning well with only the rifle in hand. He raised his rifle shoulder high, aimed at the men working on steam and water lines and around the boiler battery, and fired repeatedly. The men ran away from him and away from the well. However, one smart fellow counted the number of times Grace raised the gun to fire and when he surmised the rifle magazine must be empty (the noise of the shots was lost in the roar of the fire) he made signs to the other men to "go get him." Several hundred men grabbed clubs, wrenches, and shovels and gave chase. Grace threw down his rifle and ran toward the blazing well. A soldier on guard near the well tried to stop him. Grace grappled the soldier and tried to take his rifle, but the soldier held on and in the struggle the gun went off. Grace fell, wounded in the head. Quickly he was trussed up. His wounds were not serious so he was hustled off to jail in Tuxpam, with an armed guard.

Grace recovered. The company got him out of jail and had him sent back to the States for treatment in an institution for mental illness. About a year later, unknown to the company, he was released from the institution in the States, returned to Tampico and committed suicide in one of the local hotels by slitting his throat.

The Grace episode was indeed tragic in its consequences. But on reflection there was the lighter side, too— for example, Epley with the catsup bottle, and my blue funk when the fellow hollered, "Here he comes."

So much for what the *Chronicle* account of the Toteco fire did not relate.

International Petroleum Company's Toteco No. 4 was located some 1,200 feet south of Gulf's Toteco No. 4 on an adjoining 40 acre block. IPC's No. 4 was completed a month after Gulf's No. 4 had been brought under control.

IPC's No. 4 came in wild in a very freakish way and so the story of its taming is of considerable interest.

As I recollect, the hole was being drilled into the pay through a liner (steel casing, extending down through the master gate to near bottom) on which a secondary valve had been fixed. When the well blew in, the flow came out faster than the drilling cable, causing the latter to ball up in the recesses of the valve on top. The crew was unable to free this stuck cable so, of necessity, removed the valve from the liner amidst a spraying mess of black oil. The operation was successful but then the freak incident occurred.

Naturally, the drill crew expected and were prepared for the oil flow to come out of the liner from just below the derrick floor and shoot straight up when they had removed the valve and got the drill cable and tools out of the hole. But not so in this well. Instead the liner pipe floated up on the tremendous flow of oil—oil coming out through the liner as well as around it—until its top extended twenty feet or so above the derrick. And there it remained shooting oil hundreds of feet skyward as from a giant vertical nozzle. Evidently the liner had parted somewhere below ground from the tremendous force of the gusher against the balled up cable.

First of all the well crews tried to pull the liner out but could not. Then they attached ropes around the "floating" liner and tried pulling it back into the hole. They could easily pull it down but could not force the top of the liner below the master valve seat. They were also unsuccessful in backing off the top joint of the liner because of the oil flowing both inside and outside the pipe. This was indeed something new in wild wells.

After repeated attempts to get the loose pipe out, or in or off, a young Irish geologist (Dana McKenna) had a novel idea. He talked with the local management and they gave him a free hand. So, McKenna went to the field warehouse and obtained three long triangular-pyramid shaped coarse-toothed steel files. These he took to the shops, where the butts were cut off and drilled to receive a threaded, small-diameter, round iron rod. The rods were about twelve feet long, with an eye ring on the end opposite the threads. When all was ready, the three rods with triangular files screwed on—not too tightly—were carried to the rig.

The crew pulled down the liner until they were sure the first pipe collar was below the master gate seat. While the liner was held in that position the three "spears" were lowered into the well so that the points were below the main valve and also below the first collar of the liner. The spear points were now between the outer wall of the liner pipe and the inner wall of the master casing. Wooden mallets were used to hammer home the spears. When the spear points were tight the rods were unscrewed, the top joint of the liner bucked off, and the seat of the master gate was closed over the top of the wedged liner. Thus IPC's wild one was tamed.

Incidentally, the loose but now wedged liner was never removed from the well. Instead the company rigged up top connections on the master gate and drilled a hole in the master gate seat with a rose bit, through which the well was produced until salt water encroachment replaced the oil.

Because of the proximity of this well to those of my company, I remained on the job as an observer during the control effort. However, as so often happens, I had better sense for others than for myself. I nearly lost my life, needlessly and carelessly.

One late afternoon, before the well was brought under control, I started back to camp alone. The wild well and the camp were located on little hills about a half mile apart. Everything around the well for a mile or more was wet with wind-carried oil and gas spray. However, this day there was no wind of consequence. The air was humid and heavy. The sky was overcast and rain was imminent. So, I set off down a narrow foot trail to camp by the short cut through a swale of brush. When I was well into the brush I suddenly realized I was being gassed with the low-lying H_2S oil fumes. It flashed over my mind that if I collapsed in that brush-lined trail in this low spot I would have had it, for keeps. I started to run and fought to remain conscious. Somehow I made it to the muddy road on the camp side of the swale before I fell flat. Fortunately, as I fell my head turned so that my nose and mouth were out of the mud and water. How long I lay there I do not know. Finally, my senses cleared as the fresh gas-free air revived me, and I staggered up and into the camp—still groggy and very wet and muddy all over, but alive.

17

Bloodless Revolution

On the *Cinco de Mayo* in 1920 strong Rebel forces moved up from the south against the Federal troops in Tampico. The revolutionists had several field pieces of artillery which were placed at strategic points along the Panuco River bank opposite the Fiscal Wharf and Custom House, where the Federals had assembled. According to the rumors in town, the Rebel forces were better armed and greatly outnumbered the Federals. It was also rumored that a large sum of money had been cached in the Custom House. Apparently the Rebels not only wanted to capture Mexico's largest port city but hoped to get the national funds.

The situation among the residents of Tampico was tense and grew more so as word came that another strong force of Rebels was moving in on the city, along the rail lines, from the west and north. If these Rebel forces could join up, the fate of the small Federal garrison looked bad. They were in no position, either with men or arms, to withstand a long siege.

226

It was generally the opinion that if a fight ensued the Federals must surely lose. They could escape only by land over one main road which led away from the city to the northwest. The road ran between the converging rail lines and passed through the Aguila and Colonia colonies, where most of the foreigners had homes. Should such an escape be attempted after a battle, everyone felt the defeated soldiers would pillage, burn and rape the foreigners as they retreated through the colonies.

American gunboats lay in the Panuco River between the Custom House and the Rebels on the south bank. These boats had stripped for action, with their guns trained on both forces. Uncle Sam evidently was prepared to protect civilian life and private property in the city.

Tampico was crowded with thousands of Mexican refugees from the outlying country. For the most part, these refugees had no lodging in the city—in fact, no place to lay their heads under shelter. Men, women and children were everywhere in the streets and doorways. They stood or sat silently huddled in their serapes, looking scared and hungry and confused, waiting for they knew not what.

The city market place was open, but stores were closed and windows shuttered. All offices had closed and sent their help home. All over the city there was a loud silence as the populace waited for the first shots to be exchanged.

During the lull I had gone out to the Aguila Colony to look after my family. My wife had not yet come downstairs following the birth of our second child, a daughter, born on April 18th in our home. A local American doctor had attended and we now had the competent services of a lovely young American nurse from New Orleans, who happened to be visiting friends in Tampico at the time.

Naturally, all the foreigners in the colonies were nervous and jittery. In our family the tension was terriffc because if worse came to worse (with defeated soldiers, seeking revenge on Gringos by pillage, fire and rape, rampaging through the colonies) we could not suddenly flee. The only escape would have to be by launch before the rabble arrived—out the Chairel Lagoon down the Tamesi and into the Panuco River, thence, downstream, past the Fiscal Wharf to one of the oil company terminals near the mouth of the Panuco, where a U.S. tanker was loading.

It was agreed that such an exodus was best while there was time to properly escort my wife and children to the water's edge for embarkation. Accordingly, I ordered the company speed boat by telephone through to Prieto. Soon as this boat was sighted, my wife, the nurse, our 2 year old boy, the baby and my friend (Bill Cook, assistant general agent of the Mexican Gulf Oil Company) and his wife were taken by car down the bluff and loaded on board the little speed boat. Away they went, so loaded down that the boat had only a few inches of free board at the stern. It was agreed that I would close up the house and await word from Cook that my family had safely arrived at their destination.

An hour or so went by without any word. Although I heard no sounds of gunfire from the city I feared something might have happened to the speed boat en route. Maybe it had been swamped or maybe they had been shot by either side. With all these and many more apprehensions in mind—all the time condemning myself for not having gone along to look after my family—I got into our car and headed back to the city.

When I arrived I found the central plaza crowded with civilians standing and gaping at the Custom House. I pushed my way through the mob to the front ranks and there, of all people, was Bill—calmly watching the water front where the battle was momentarily expected to begin.

I grabbed him and shouted, "Where are the women, my son and the baby? Are they safe and why didn't you phone me at home as agreed?"

Nonchalantly he replied, "They are all safe and well and on board the Freeport Company's tanker, but in the excitement I forgot to telephone you."

I was furious and felt like clobbering him for his casualness. Probably I would have, but just then a steamer whistled as it moved away from the wharf and slowly gathered speed downstream. Then came a burst of rifle fire from the Rebel side and a volley from the steamer. Sporadic rifle fire kept up until the steamer was out of range. In the city's main plaza all was pandemonium—the crowds danced and shouted and sang. It had dawned on the people that the Federals had escaped on the steamer with the money, and without serious battle.

The Rebels quickly swarmed into the city and took over the local government. Strangely enough, they were well-ordered troops, and the changeover was quiet and uneventful. The next day, Tampico was wide open for business as usual and my family returned home.

My wife told me all about the excitement of their boat trip downstream to the tanker. Apparently, the party had all been in a holiday mood as they sped along the Panuco. Their boat had passed close alongside the American gunboat, directly beneath the guns trained on the Custom House. They waved at the astonished sailors and marines as they went by. No one had fired at their passing craft, so far as they knew. At the Freeport Terminal they had been made very comfortable and welcome.

A few days later the local colony arranged a dance to which the officers of the American gunboat were invited. One of the young officers had dated our nurse. He arrived at our home in his tropical dress uniform—a fine looking, upstanding representative of Uncle Sam's best. We stood around talking while waiting for the nurse. During the congenial parley, the young officer paid his respects to the American colony of Tampico in glowing terms, but with one exception.

"What is that exception," my wife asked.

"Well," he said, "the other day when the battle was momentarily expected our ship was prepared for action and our crew was all at its several battle stations, when lo and behold there came speeding by, right under our guns, a boat load of crazy American women and children on an excursion. They waved at us and laughingly shouted greeting to our nonplused crew."

With that remark my wife blew up. She said, "We were those people—we were not excursionists but were fleeing as fast as we could to an oil tanker downstream."

Just then our nurse appeared in her party dress looking mighty sweet and pretty. The young naval officer looked at the nurse and then at my wife, evidently recognizing both as being among the "crazy" Americans in the boat. He grinned and said, "Well, what I didn't know then I now understand. Please accept my sincere apology." With that we all laughed.

The young folks went on off to the dance, while my wife and I sat quietly—thankful to be home with our two children, all safe and well in spite of revolution.

18

Expropriation:
Mexican Takeover

When the Conquistadores conquered pagan Mexico, all land and minerals were declared to be the property of Spain. During the next four centuries most land titles were referred to old Spanish grants and all minerals were considered the property of the nation. However, petroleum and other hydrocarbons were not classified as minerals by either the Spaniards or their successors until after the fall of Porfirio Diaz. Prior to that time, title to the petroleum and other hydrocarbons went with the surface of the land. Because of that fact, when oil and gas were discovered in commercial quantities in Mexico the oil companies acquired their rights to explore and exploit the underground by leases made with the current landowners. Under the terms of these private leases oil royalties and annual rents were paid to the private owners—as in the United States—and the government, either local, state or federal, derived no direct income therefrom. Under such conditions and legal procedure the great oil dynasties of the British, Dutch and American companies grew and flourished in Mexico from 1900 to 1917.

Then on May 1, 1917, a new Mexican Constitution was enacted in which Article 27 stated, in part:

In the nation is vested direct ownership of all minerals or substances which in veins, masses or beds constitute deposits whose nature is different from the components of the land, such as minerals from which metals and metalloids used for industrial purposes are extracted, beds of precious stones, rock salt and salt lakes formed directly by marine waters, products derived from the decomposition of rocks, when their exploitation requires underground working, phosphates which may be used as fertilizers; *solid mineral fuels, petroleums and all hydrocarbons, solid, liquid or gaseous.**

In February 1918 the Mexican government issued a decree taxing oil lands and contracts entered into prior to May 1, 1917. This was actually a tax on rents and royalties due under the agreements with the private land owner. A little later the government declared that private owners who had not leased their subsoil rights prior to March, 1917, or who had not themselves taken out government concessions within a specified time after that date, had lost all their rights to the petroleum and related hydrocarbons in the subsoil of the land to which they held surface title. The government further declared unequivocally that all petroleum rights under navigable waters and lakes, bays and inlets of the sea, or along their margins, as well as under all municipal lands and vacant lands were vested in the nation.

Subsequently, there were issued many decrees interpreting the provisions of Article 27 of the 1917 Mexican Constitution pertaining to oil rights, as well as various tax provisions relative to the rents and royalties acruing to

---

*The italics are mine.

the private owner of the subsoil and also decrees affecting taxes on the production and the export of crude and oil products. Still these interpretations and taxes were not in themselves confiscatory and the foreign oil companies continued to operate, though with increasing difficulty.

Coincident with the 1917 Constitution came social revolution. Landed estates were taken over by the government and parcelled out to the peons. Labor on the farm, as well as in industry, was organized. Demands for higher wages, and better working and living conditions spiraled upward at a rate far beyond the capacity of either agriculture, mine, factory, oil or business to cope with and survive.

Radical leaders obtained control of the great mining, railroad and oil labor syndicates. Strikes, both local and general, occurred and recurred from 1918 to 1938. The powerful labor syndicates virtually dominated the state and national governments. The politicians became their tool and politics their game—even the judgment of the Mexican courts was affected.

Out of the multitudinous and impossible demands of the oil syndicates came the impasse between the Mexican courts and the oil companies, which led to the famous expropriation proceedings in the spring of 1938.* The Mexican government took over all the oil properties—camps, wells, pipelines, terminals, tankage, refineries, offices, oil in storage, materials and equipment of all kinds—of all the larger foreign oil companies, except one. That one, the Mexican Gulf Oil Company, was not expropriated but continued to do business in Mexico until 1951 when it sold its properties to PEMEX, a Mexican government-owned company.

---

*To those readers who may want to learn more about Mexico's confiscation of oil properties through the "Labor Squeeze," the author recommends the book, written in laymen's language, *Two Strikes and Out,* edited by William E. McMahon, as published by Country Life Press Corporation in 1939.

Why were Gulf's Mexican properties not confiscated in 1938 along with the properties of the other foreign owned oil companies? One reason was because Gulf was not involved in any serious labor dispute in 1937-1938—its laborers were not members of the National Oil Workers Syndicate. But why were not Gulf laborers members of the National Oil Workers Syndicate, along with most of the workers of the other foreign oil companies? To find the answer to that question one must go back some eighteen years prior to expropriation.

In 1919 and 1920 there were several general strikes among oil workers. On one occasion the National Syndicate called out all the oil workers engaged at the various tanker loading terminals and refineries in the Tampico area. Thousands of laborers were idle. The oil business was all but paralyzed. By vicious threats and actual violence, the Syndicate made every effort to keep all oil labor from working—whether members of the National union or not.

At the time, I was general agent for Gulf in Mexico with offices in Tampico. Gulf had no refinery in Mexico and its sole tanker loading terminal was located at Prieto on the Panuco River about five miles upstream from the Fiscal Wharf. During those days it was the practice to transport the daily laborers required at Prieto to and from Tampico by barge. Customarily, these barges and towing tugboats departed from the Fiscal Wharf about six o'clock each weekday morning and returned about six o'clock each evening.

One morning I awakened early in my Tampico apartment, where I was living at the time with my wife and small son. The bedside clock indicated the hour was five o'clock, too early to rouse for the office. I turned over and tried to sleep, but something, some feeling, impelled me to get up, dress quickly and go down to the waterfront. I set out for the Fiscal Wharf, on foot, unarmed and alone.

I sensed there was going to be trouble at the wharf that morning and that, for some reason not clear to me, I should be there.

At that hour in the morning the main streets of Tampico were quiet. Only a few people were out, mostly headed toward the markets. The store fronts were still shuttered and hardly a street vendor was in sight. There was little sign of life except in the vicinity of the market near the canal, which separated the city from the Custom House and Fiscal Wharf. I strode down the streets from my apartment, crossed the bridge over the canal, and then made my way over the railroad tracks to the wharf. As I walked along the wide cement floored wharf—which parallels the Panuco River—I could see hundreds of laborers lining the edge of the dock. I pushed my way through the milling, but more or less friendly, mob toward the upstream end of the wharf from where our men usually embarked. Finally, I located our crew barge—a small wooden flat top dumb barge—with the *Gulfito*, our small gasoline tug, tied up alongside. One end of the barge was nuzzled up against the wharf so that our men could come aboard without undue difficulty.

I jumped onto the barge, crossed over to the tug and inquired why our 40 or 50 men had not boarded as the hour of departure was at hand. The tug captain (a Tex-Mex) said to me in English, "Jefe, the men are all there on the dock but have not come on board for fear of violence. They are being threatened by the National Oil Union strikers you see all around them." Sure enough, I could see over 500 workmen in the crowd, some with visible knives and machetes and a few with clubs and guns. As I looked shoreward, the attitude and expression of those men on the dock did not appear nearly so friendly as I had thought. In the forefront I observed Garcia, one of my company's detectives —a former intelligence officer with the Mexican government forces. I knew him personally, and called out for him to join me. He promptly jumped on board and confirmed that our men were there, ready and willing to go to work, but were scared of the mob.

I thought to myself, this is a showdown. If our men want to come and we fail to take them off safely my company will be in for serious difficulty. I quickly outlined a plan, but explained to Garcia that I was not sure it would work. He agreed it was worth a try. We would blow the tug whistle as a signal for departure and Garcia would station himself at the bow end of the barge with his coat thrown back so that his holstered gun could easily be seen. He was to prevent any non-Gulf men from jumping onto the barge. He said he knew each and everyone of our men by sight and name.

The strategy worked. Our men quickly tumbled on board the barge, but not without a deal of commotion on the dock. A few shots were fired by strikers, a few knives flashed, a stone or two fell and there were angry shouts of violence. Luckily all our men got aboard safely and no one followed. Garcia had not drawn his gun. Quickly the barge lines were thrown off and our tug backed away with the barge to midstream before turning to proceed up the river to Prieto. The yelling mob of strikers was left behind, but not before we had heard their dire threats of retaliation against our workmen.

As we slowly chugged toward Prieto, I got to wondering what might happen to these workmen when they returned to their families in Tampico that night. They could be in serious trouble. Someone might be killed. With these ugly thoughts in mind, as soon as we arrived at Prieto I talked with the superintendent and his staff, told him what had happened and asked for his advice. After considerable debate, it was decided not to return the workmen to Tampico until the trouble had blown over. The workmen all

agreed, provided we would undertake to protect their families. Garcia said he would personally visit each family and would have his men, in co-operation with the Tampico police, see to it that they were not molested.

That done, the superintendent had a number of tents erected along the railroad right of way, where it crossed our terminal property, and cots and food were marshalled for the workmen. Armed guards were stationed around the tents, day and night, in case the belligerent strikers should make a sortie out from town along the tracks.

Several days went by and still the general strike was on, involving almost every other oil terminal up and down the river. After a week, our workmen made it known they wanted to be with their families—would the company bring them out to Prieto? This request called for a major decision as to whether or not the company should assume responsibility over the lives and welfare of the workmen's families. Again, after consultation it was agreed that, since these workmen had stood by us, the company could now do no less than stand by them. So, within a few days all their families and their chattels had been transported from Tampico to our tent camp at Prieto.

As the strike continued on and on, it became evident that we must consider what had started out as a temporary tent colony to be a permanent housing problem. The pros and cons of this phase of the matter were considered at length, but finally all concerned were unanimously in favor of permanent company housing for workmen and their families.

As soon as possible the tents were replaced with wooden buildings. It was crude housing compared to present day standards but nonetheless those first houses at Prieto were vastly better than the shacks and hovels in which our workmen's families had previously lived in the fever-ridden slums of Tampico. At Prieto, there was good air and plenty of room for the children and the pigs, chickens and pets. The families of our Mexican workmen had better living at Prieto than they had ever had before. They were happy and happy workmen make the best workmen, the world over.

As the years rolled by the provisional wooden houses were replaced with new modern cottages, complete with little lawns and a private backyard for flowers, animals and fowls, which all Mexican workers love. The families of those non-striking workmen of 1919 eventually grew up. Many of the girls married and moved away. However, most of the sons sought employment with Gulf at Prieto or elsewhere in Mexico.

Although I was transferred from Mexico at the end of 1922, I happened to be in Mexico City in 1951 when the sale of the Mexican Gulf Oil Co. properties was consummated with PEMEX. I asked about our old Mexican employees and was told that in the course of the thirty years many left the company for one reason or another, some had died and others had been retired on pension. Every man who had been with the company for twenty years or more was offered retirement with pension if he desired. I was highly pleased to learn that among these who now sought retirement were many of the same men who had been "barged" from Tampico to Prieto that eventful day during the general strike of the National Syndicate of Oil Workers.

I have no way of proving my point at this late date, but I am personally convinced that at least one reason Gulf's Mexican personnel never joined the National Unions was because Gulf looked after its Mexican workmen during and after the general strike which paralyzed the industry for many weeks in and around Tampico during 1919 and 1920. So it happened that Gulf was not involved in any serious labor disputes at the time of expropriation; hence, Gulf was one of the very few foreign-owned oil companies not expropriated by the Mexican government.

My only excuse for injecting "Expropriation" into these tales is to admit that the 1919 strike episode was, for me, an important and never-to-be-forgotten lesson in labor relations. As far as I know this story has never before been told.

19

The Tampico Tribune

"Tampico's Best Advertising Medium" (so claimed by its versatile editor and publisher, C. McAnderson) was read by the entire English speaking population of Tampico and the oil fields for some 30 years from about 1912. This weekly newspaper specialized in producing timely local news during a period of Mexican history when political events, social unrest, revolution and spectacular incidents in and around the oil fields were exciting and frequent occurrences. During much of this period of censorship, irregular mails and poor telegraph service, the English speaking public leaned heavily on the *Tribune* for news. There were times when this bold little press was the only source of news of the outside world.

Through the columns of the *Tampico Tribune* the local community made its plea for support of the Liberty Loan drives, the American Chamber of Commerce of Tampico, the American School Association of Tampico, Young Men's Christian Association, Chairel Outing Club and numerous other civic and patriotic undertakings. It was one of two English language newspapers in Mexico, the other being the *Mexican Herald* published in Mexico City.

The *Tribune* may never have won a prize for its editorials or makeup, but it should have been awarded a medal for consistent enterprise and realistic reporting, sometimes in the face of serious threats and reprisals from the Federal and Rebel authorities.

Mac (McAnderson) became an institution. He had on his staff a number of young, fearless reporters to search out and bring in live news. One of these, who later became famous as a columnist and author, was (Henry) Lee Shippey.

Shippey was a correspondent in Mexico in 1920 and then for two years was associated with McAnderson as editor of the *Tribune*. I got to know him very well in those days. He helped immeasurably in promoting the American Chamber of Commerce, the YMCA, the Chairel Outing Club and the American School. Shippey quit newspapering in Tampico in 1922 for, as he wrote his mother, "We've saved enough money to come back to the States and buy a shack. The stork's coming and we don't want to meet him in Mexico." For several years he tried free lance writing for *Collier's, American, Post* and *Mercury*. Finally, in 1927, he joined the *Los Angeles Times* and soon was internationally known as editor of the "Lee Side O'L.A." column.

Coincidently, while a columnist, Shippey wrote a score or more of books—homey novels of California, the countryside and family life. I treasure four of these books for their simple, homespun logic and humor—*Where Nothing Ever Happens* (1935), *The Great American Family* (1938), *If We Only Had Money* (1939), *It's An Old California Custom* (1948). In the first named book appears this endorsement:

To Charles W. Hamilton—who helped me with many a good story when I was a reporter in Tampico and he was one of the men who made it, for the time, the capital of the oil world.

Sincerely,

2/26/35   Lee Shippey

I had not seen Lee Shippey for nearly 20 years when we met again in Los Angeles. We had a grand chat about the old Tampico days over lunch in his club. He was then quite blind but still as vigorous as ever, doing his daily column and writing novels on the side. Our talk was very personal and most friendly—off the record—or so I thought. I was surprised a few days later to notice reference to our meeting in his "Lee Side O'L.A." column. I felt complimented by what he said even though his reporting was somewhat exaggerated. Here is part of his column as it appeared in the *Los Angeles Times,* December 6, 1940:

Romance of Oil

C. W. Hamilton, Vice-President of the Gulf Oil Corp. of New York was here to visit his mother, Mrs. Ella W. Hamilton, this week. When I was a reporter in Tampico, Mex., Mr. Hamilton was made local manager there for the Mexican Gulf Oil Co. Tampico was then the wildest boom town in the world. Rivers of black gold were being discovered every day. Men who arrived as tool dressers rose to be millionaires in a few years, while others went to hell because they could not withstand the temptations on every side. Truck drivers were making $350 (gold) a month plus board and room and laundry. If a bum stopped you on the street you never thought of giving him less than a dollar. Ten thousand swaggering, daredevil Americans and English were there who worked hard by day and caroused hard by night. And many of them—including some in high places—were just such liars as you find in any loud, swashbuckling crew. But Hamilton was quiet, unassertive and definitely reliable. When executives of other companies tried to put things over on me I went to Hamilton and got the truth.

20

It's a Small World

My first trip to Mexico occurred in mid-1912 and one of my last was in early 1951. During that span of 39 years my business as geologist and executive of oil companies took me all over the Americas, Europe and the Middle East. I met many interesting people in all walks of life in many different countries, sometimes under strange circumstances. Often, I found that new friends were mutual acquaintances of old friends. As the years roll by, it seems that, the wider the travel and the longer the trail, the smaller the globe. A case in point is the following story.

The Youngs and the Hamiltons first met in Tampico as young married folks back in 1918, or thereabouts. Sometime after both families had left Mexico they were again closely associated through the same business connections. Both resided for many years in New York City until the Youngs were transferred to Texas. Because of their mutual friendship and their mutual love of Mexico and the Mexicans, the Youngs and Hamiltons embarked together on a sort of farewell trip to the land south of the Rio Grande. Both couples were thrilled over the possibility of now being able to travel freely around the country without fear of bandits or revolutionists and to visit places which were inaccessible to them thirty years ago.

We arrived in Mexico City in January, 1951, and, as soon as we had settled in La Reforma, began to make contact with such of our old acquaintances of yesteryear as resided in the city. Among others, we got in touch with General Harry Johnson, formerly an employee of the oil company we were still associated with. The General had been stationed in Mexico for some time as head of the Aftosa campaign. The campaign was now winding up its affairs and as a result there was a temporary surplus of autos and drivers in the Aftosa car pool. One of those cars and a driver was put at our disposal for the duration of our stay, through the courtesy of the General and his operating staff.

The following morning the doorman at La Reforma told us that our Chevrolet and chauffeur were awaiting us. Juan, the chauffeur, proved to be a pleasant mannered, middle-aged fellow. After making our salutations in Spanish, we entered the car—the Youngs and my wife took the rear seat and I was up front with Juan. Soon we were off to visit the pyramids. En route I acted as tour guide. I had made several trips out to the pyramids years ago, and accordingly explained (in English) the several points of interest as we passed by in the auto. All our conversation with Juan was in Spanish.

To my surpirse, Juan turned to me as we were returning to the city over the same route and said in very passable English, "Mr. Hamilton, pardon me but what you told your friends about that building (the one we had just passed) is not quite correct." Then Juan told us what the building really was.

After my moment of confusion I said to Juan, "Where did you learn your English?"

He replied, "Asia Minor."

"But Juan, you are Mexican, how does it happen you learned English in Asia Minor?" I asked.

"Senor," said Juan, "I was born in Asia Minor and only became a Mexican citizen when I came to this country."

Juan told us that he had been born in Armenia, his real name was Toros Demirdjian, and that he had moved to Lebanon as a young man. There for some years he was a chauffeur and mechanic for Dr. and Mrs. Bayard Dodge, then President of the American University at Beirut. When I told Juan that my wife and I had known the Dodges intimately for many years he was overjoyed. He said Dr. Dodge had given him an introductory letter, "to whom it may concern," prior to his migration to America.

The following is an extract of a letter I wrote to Dr. Bayard Dodge, then in Princeton, New Jersey, under date of Feb. 16, 1951, after our return home.

He (Toros Demirdjian) was a chauffeur and mechanic for you and your wife at the American University more than 25 years ago—(he) presently lives at Corregidora 85-1 Mexico, D. F. John (Juan) proved to be an excellent driver and extremely courteous. When he found out that we knew you and your wife and that our son was now teaching there, he clung to us like a blood brother. He repeatedly requested that I get in touch with you upon my return and to remind you that some day he hoped to visit the States and have an opportunity to see you and your good wife. Incidentally, he was so proud of his relationship with your family that he brought me a letter which you at one time wrote him and also brought me pictures of the several members of his family. I am enclosing herewith a note received from him under date of February 12th in which he refers to you and his hope of seeing you and your wife in the near future. I think nothing would give "John" more pleasure than to receive a note from you at your convenience.

Some weeks after that letter was written I learned from Dr. Dodge that he remembered Juan very well and often wondered what had become of him—furthermore, that he was writing to Juan in Mexico City, as Juan had suggested.

This tale has no historic significance and is more commonplace than otherwise. Still, it is rather unusual to learn that one's Mexican chauffeur is in fact from Asia Minor and that his old friends in Beirut are your own good friends.

Yes indeed, it is a small world.